TO

Paul

FROM

Tom

DATE

2010 – A New Life!

PRAYERS
&PROMISES

FOR MEN

Parable
3563 Empleo
St. San Luis Obispo, CA 93401

The quoted ideas expressed in this book (but not Scripture verses) are not, in all cases, exact quotations, as some have been edited for clarity and brevity. In all cases, the author has attempted to maintain the speaker's original intent. In some cases, quoted material for this book was obtained from secondary sources, primarily print media. While every effort was made to ensure the accuracy of these sources, the accuracy cannot be guaranteed. For additions, deletions, corrections, or clarifications in future editions of this text, please write Parable.

The Holy Bible, King James Version

The Holy Bible, New King James Version (NKJV) Copyright © 1982 by Thomas Nelson, Inc. Used by permission.

New Century Version®. (NCV) Copyright © 1987, 1988, 1991 by Word Publishing, a division of Thomas Nelson, Inc. All rights reserved. Used by permission.

The Holman Christian Standard Bible™ (HCSB) Copyright © 1999, 2000, 2001 by Holman Bible Publishers. Used by permission.

The Holy Bible, New International Version®. (NIV) Copyright © 1973, 1978, 1984 International Bible Society. Used by permission of Zondervan. All rights reserved.

The Holy Bible. New Living Translation (NLT) copyright © 1996 Tyndale Charitable Trust. Used by permission of Tyndale House Publishers.

Scripture taken from The Message. (MSG) Copyright © 1993, 1994, 1995, 1996, 2000, 2001, 2002. Used by permission of NavPress Publishing Group.

The New American Standard Bible®, (NASB) Copyright © 1960, 1962, 1963, 1968, 1971, 1972, 1973, 1975, 1977, 1995 by The Lockman Foundation. Used by permission.

Cover Design by Kim Russell / Wahoo Designs
Page Layout by Bart Dawson

ISBN-13 978-1-58334-439-2

ISBN-10 1-58334-439-X

Printed in the United States of America

PRAYERS
&PROMISES

FOR MEN

TABLE OF CONTENTS

INTRODUCTION

God's Holy Word contains promises upon which we, as Christians, can and must depend. The Bible is a priceless gift from our Creator; it is a tool that God intends for us to use in every aspect of our lives. Yet sometimes, when the demands of everyday life threaten to overwhelm us, we may fail to consult God's Word as often as we should. If you find yourself in that predicament, this book is intended to help.

You hold in your hands a collection of Bible verses, inspirational quotations, essays, and prayers. This text is intended as an inspirational reminder of the opportunities and possibilities that await you every day of your life.

God's promises are eternal and unchanging. But, as every man knows, life in today's fast-paced world can be so demanding and so confusing that it becomes easy to forget God's blessings and His mercy. This book invites you to slow down and take inventory of the joys and blessings that God offers to all His children, including you.

The ideas in this text are intended to be powerful reminders—reminders of God's commandments, reminders of God's promises, and reminders of God's blessings. May these pages be a blessing to you, and may you, in turn, be a blessing to those whom God has seen fit to place along your path.

ABILITY

Now there are different gifts, but the same Spirit. There are different ministries, but the same Lord.

1 Corinthians 12:4-5 HCSB

Every generous act and every perfect gift is from above, coming down from the Father of lights.

James 1:17 HCSB

Each one has his own gift from God, one in this manner and another in that.

1 Corinthians 7:7 NKJV

Do not neglect the spiritual gift that is within you . . . .

1 Timothy 4:14 NASB

God has given gifts to each of you from his great variety of spiritual gifts. Manage them well so that God's generosity can flow through you.

1 Peter 4:10 NLT

God knew precisely what He was doing when He gave you a unique set of abilities and opportunities. And now, God wants you to use those talents for the glory of His kingdom. So here's the big question: will you choose to use your talents or not?

Your Heavenly Father wants you to be a faithful steward of the gifts He has given you. But you live in a society that may encourage you to do otherwise. You face countless temptations to squander your time, your resources, and your talents. So you must be keenly aware of the inevitable distractions that can waste your time, your energy, and your opportunities.

God has blessed you with many opportunities to serve Him, and He has given you every tool you need to do so. Today, accept this challenge: value the talent that God has given you, nourish it, make it grow, and share it with the world, beginning now.

You are the only person on earth who can use your ability.

Zig Ziglar

Dear Lord, I thank You for the abilities and the opportunities You have given me. Let me treasure them, let me nurture them, and let me use them for Your glory as I walk in the footsteps of Your Son. Amen

ABUNDANCE

I am come that they might have life, and that they might have it more abundantly.

John 10:10 KJV

But this I say, He which soweth sparingly shall reap also sparingly; and he which soweth bountifully shall reap also bountifully.

2 Corinthians 9:6 KJV

My cup runneth over. Surely goodness and mercy shall follow me all the days of my life: and I will dwell in the house of the LORD for ever.

Psalm 23:5-6 KJV

Ask and it will be given to you; seek and you will find; knock and the door will be opened to you. For everyone who asks receives; he who seeks finds; and to him who knocks, the door will be opened.

Matthew 7:7-8 NIV

His master replied, "Well done, good and faithful servant! You have been faithful with a few things; I will put you in charge of many things. Come and share your master's happiness!"

Matthew 25:21 NIV

When Jesus talks of the abundant life, is He talking about material riches or earthly fame? Hardly. The Son of God came to this world not to give it prosperity, but to give it salvation. Thankfully for Christians, our Savior's abundance is both spiritual and eternal; it never falters—even if we do—and it never dies. We need only to open our hearts to Him, and His grace becomes ours.

God's gifts are available to all, but they are not guaranteed; those gifts must be claimed by those who choose to follow Christ. As believers, we are free to accept God's gifts, or not; that choice, and the consequences that result from it, are ours and ours alone.

As we go about our daily lives, may we accept God's promise of spiritual abundance, and may we share it with a world in desperate need of the Master's healing touch.

———

The only way you can experience abundant life is to surrender your plans to Him.

Charles Stanley

———

Heavenly Father, thank You for the abundant life that is mine through Christ Jesus. Guide me according to Your will, and help me to be a worthy servant in all that I say and do. Give me courage, Lord, to claim the rewards You have promised, and when I do, let the glory be Yours. Amen

God's Promises About . . .

ACCEPTANCE

A man's heart plans his way, but the Lord determines his steps.

Proverbs 16:9 HCSB

For everything created by God is good, and nothing should be rejected if it is received with thanksgiving.

1 Timothy 4:4 HCSB

Should we accept only good from God and not adversity?

Job 2:10 HCSB

Come to terms with God and be at peace; in this way good will come to you.

Job 22:21 HCSB

Sheathe your sword! Should I not drink the cup that the Father has given Me?

John 18:11 HCSB

I f you're like most men, you like being in control. Period. You want things to happen according to your wishes and according to your timetable. But sometimes, God has other plans . . . and He always has the final word.

The American theologian Reinhold Niebuhr composed a profoundly simple verse that came to be known as the Serenity Prayer: "God, grant me the serenity to accept the things I cannot change, the courage to change the things I can, and the wisdom to know the difference." Niebuhr's words are far easier to recite than they are to live by.

So if you've encountered unfortunate circumstances that are beyond your power to control, accept those circumstances . . . and trust God. When you do, you can be comforted in the knowledge that your Creator is both loving and wise, and that He understands His plans perfectly, even when you do not.

Acceptance is resting in God's goodness, believing that He has all things under His control.

Charles Swindoll

Lord, when I am discouraged, give me hope. When I am impatient, give me peace. When I face circumstances that I cannot change, give me a spirit of acceptance. In all things great and small, let me trust in You, Dear Lord, knowing that You are the Giver of life and the Giver of all things good, today and forever. Amen

ACCEPTING CHRIST

For God loved the world in this way: He gave His only Son, so that everyone who believes in Him will not perish but have eternal life.

John 3:16 HCSB

Yet we know that no one is justified by the works of the law but by faith in Jesus Christ. And we have believed in Christ Jesus, so that we might be justified by faith in Christ and not by the works of the law, because by the works of the law no human being will be justified.

Galatians 2:16 HCSB

And we have seen and testify that the Father has sent the Son as Savior of the world.

1 John 4:14 NKJV

God wanted to make known to those among the Gentiles the glorious wealth of this mystery, which is Christ in you, the hope of glory.

Colossians 1:27 HCSB

God loves you. Period. And His affection for you is deeper and more profound than you can imagine. God's love for you is so great that He sent His only Son to this earth to die for your sins and to offer you the priceless gift of eternal life. Now, you must decide whether or not to accept God's gift. Will you ignore it or embrace it? Will you return it or neglect it? Will you accept Christ or not? The decision, of course, is yours and yours alone, and the decision has eternal consequences. Accept God's gift: Accept Christ.

To accept Christ is to know the meaning of the words "as he is, so are we in this world." We accept his friends as our friends, his enemies as our enemies, his ways as our ways, his rejection as our rejection, his cross as our cross, his life as our life, and his future as our future.

A. W. Tozer

Dear Lord, when You invited me to be part of Your family, I said yes. I confessed that Jesus was my Lord and Savior, and You saved me. I choose, this day, to live in such a way that others, especially my family, might also accept Christ as their Savior and that they might see my love for You reflected through my words and my deeds. Amen

ADVERSITY

Be of good cheer; I have overcome the world.

John 16:33 KJV

No discipline seems pleasant at the time, but painful. Later on, however, it produces a harvest of righteousness and peace for those who have been trained by it.

Hebrews 12:11 NIV

For though a righteous man falls seven times, he rises again . . . .

Proverbs 24:16 NIV

The Lord lifts the burdens of those bent beneath their loads. The Lord loves the righteous.

Psalm 146:8 NLT

Come to me, all you who are weary and burdened, and I will give you rest. Take my yoke upon you and learn from me, for I am gentle and humble in heart, and you will find rest for your souls. For my yoke is easy and my burden is light.

Matthew 11:28-30 NIV

The times that try your soul are also the times that build your character. During the darker days of life, you can learn lessons that are impossible to learn during sunny, happier days. Times of adversity can—and should—be times of intense spiritual and personal growth. But God will not force you to learn the lessons of adversity. You must learn them for yourself.

The next time Old Man Trouble knocks on your door, remember that he has lessons to teach. So turn away Mr. Trouble as quickly as you can, but as you're doing so, don't forget to learn his lessons. And remember: the trouble with trouble isn't just the trouble it causes; it's also the trouble we cause ourselves if we ignore the things that trouble has to teach. Got that? Then please don't forget it!

Throughout history, when God's people found themselves facing impossible odds, they reminded themselves of God's limitless power.

Bill Hybels

Dear Heavenly Father, You are my strength and my protector. When I am troubled, You comfort me. When I am discouraged, You lift me up. In times of adversity, let me trust Your plan and Your will for my life. Your love is infinite, as is Your wisdom. Whatever my circumstances, Dear Lord, let me always give the praise and the thanks and the glory to You. Amen

ANGER

And the servant of the Lord must not strive; but be gentle unto all men, apt to teach, patient; in meekness instructing those that oppose themselves . . . .

2 Timothy 2:24-25 KJV

Let all bitterness, and wrath, and anger, and clamor, and evil speaking, be put away from you, with all malice: and be ye kind one to another, tender-hearted, forgiving one another, even as God for Christ's sake hath forgiven you.

Ephesians 4:31-32 KJV

But I tell you that men will have to give account on the day of judgment for every careless word they have spoken. For by your words you will be acquitted, and by your words you will be condemned.

Matthew 12:36-37 NIV

But I tell you that anyone who is angry with his brother is subject to judgment.

Matthew 5:22 NIV

A patient man has great understanding, but a quick-tempered man displays folly.

Proverbs 14:29 NIV

Sometimes, anger is appropriate. Even Jesus became angry when confronted with the moneychangers in the temple. On occasion, you, like Jesus, will confront evil, and when you do, you may respond as He did: vigorously and without reservation. But, more often than not, your frustrations will be of the more mundane variety. As long as you live here on earth, you will face countless opportunities to lose your temper over small, relatively insignificant events: a traffic jam, a spilled cup of coffee, an inconsiderate comment, a broken promise. When you are tempted to lose your temper over the minor inconveniences of life, don't. Turn away from anger, hatred, bitterness, and regret. Turn instead to God.

———

Anger breeds remorse in the heart, discord in the home, bitterness in the community, and confusion in the state.

Billy Graham

———

Lord, I can be so impatient, and I can become so angry. Calm me down, Lord, and give me the maturity and the wisdom to be a patient, forgiving Christian friend. Just as You have forgiven me, Father, let me forgive others so that I can follow the example of Your Son. Amen

ASKING GOD

If you need wisdom—if you want to know what God wants you to do—ask him, and he will gladly tell you. He will not resent your asking.

James 1:5 NLT

From now on, whatever you request along the lines of who I am and what I am doing, I'll do it. That's how the Father will be seen for who he is in the Son. I mean it. Whatever you request in this way, I'll do.

John 14:13-14 MSG

You did not choose me, but I chose you and appointed you to go and bear fruit—fruit that will last. Then the Father will give you whatever you ask in my name.

John 15:16 NIV

You fathers—if your children ask for a fish, do you give them a snake instead? Or if they ask for an egg, do you give them a scorpion? Of course not! If you sinful people know how to give good gifts to your children, how much more will your heavenly Father give the Holy Spirit to those who ask him.

Luke 11:11-13 NLT

Sometimes, amid the demands and the frustrations of everyday life, we forget to slow ourselves down long enough to talk with God. Instead of turning our thoughts and prayers to Him, we rely upon our own resources. Instead of praying for strength and courage, we seek to manufacture it within ourselves. Instead of asking God for guidance, we depend only upon our own limited wisdom. The results of such behaviors are unfortunate and, on occasion, tragic.

Are you in need? Ask God to sustain you. Are you troubled? Take your worries to Him in prayer. Are you weary? Seek God's strength. In all things great and small, seek God's wisdom and His grace. He hears your prayers, and He will answer. All you must do is ask.

———

Don't be afraid to ask your heavenly Father for anything you need. Indeed, nothing is too small for God's attention or too great for his power.

Dennis Swanberg

———

Lord, You are the giver of all things good. When I am in need, I come to You in prayer. You know the desires of my heart, Lord. Grant them, I ask, yet not my will but Your will be done. Amen

God's Promises About . . .

ATTITUDE

There is one thing I always do. Forgetting the past and straining toward what is ahead, I keep trying to reach the goal and get the prize for which God called me . . . .

Philippians 3:13–14 NCV

For God has not given us a spirit of fear, but of power and of love and of a sound mind.

2 Timothy 1:7 NLT

Keep your eyes focused on what is right, and look straight ahead to what is good.

Proverbs 4:25 NCV

A miserable heart means a miserable life; a cheerful heart fills the day with a song.

Proverbs 15:15 MSG

You were taught, with regard to your former way of life, to put off your old self, which is being corrupted by its deceitful desires; to be made new in the attitude of your minds; and to put on the new self, created to be like God in true righteousness and holiness.

Ephesians 4:22-24 NIV

What's your attitude today? Are you fearful, angry, bored, or worried? Are you worried more about pleasing your friends than about pleasing your God? Are you confused, bitter, or pessimistic? If so, God wants to have a little talk with you.

God created you in His own image, and He wants you to experience joy and abundance. But, God will not force His joy upon you; you must claim it for yourself. So today, and every day hereafter, celebrate this life that God has given you. Think optimistically about yourself and your future. Give thanks to the One who has given you everything, and trust in your heart that He wants to give you so much more.

Attitude is all-important. Let the soul take a quiet attitude of faith and love toward God, and from there on, the responsibility is God's. He will make good on His commitments.

A. W. Tozer

Lord, I pray for an attitude that is Christlike as I trust completely in the promises of Your Holy Word. And whatever circumstances I face, whether good or bad, triumphal or tragic, empower me to reflect a God-honoring, Christlike attitude of optimism, faith, and love for You . . . today, tomorrow, and forever. Amen

CHEERFULNESS

Be cheerful. Keep things in good repair. Keep your spirits up. Think in harmony. Be agreeable. Do all that, and the God of love and peace will be with you for sure.

2 Corinthians 13:11 MSG

God loves a cheerful giver.

2 Corinthians 9:7 NIV

Jacob said, "For what a relief it is to see your friendly smile. It is like seeing the smile of God!"

Genesis 33:10 NLT

Do everything readily and cheerfully—no bickering, no second-guessing allowed! Go out into the world uncorrupted, a breath of fresh air in this squalid and polluted society. Provide people with a glimpse of good living and of the living God. Carry the light-giving Message into the night.

Philippians 2:14-15 MSG

Is anyone happy? Let him sing songs of praise.

James 5:13 NIV

Cheerfulness is a gift that we give to others and to ourselves. And, as believers who have been saved by a risen Christ, why shouldn't we be cheerful? The answer, of course, is that we have every reason to honor our Savior with joy in our hearts, smiles on our faces, and words of celebration on our lips.

Few things in life are more sad, or, for that matter, more absurd, than grumpy Christians. Christ promises us lives of abundance and joy if we accept His love and His grace. Yet sometimes, even the most righteous among us are beset by fits of ill temper and frustration. During these moments, we may not feel like turning our thoughts and prayers to Christ, but if we seek to gain perspective and peace, that's precisely what we must do.

Are you a cheerful Christian? You should be! And what is the best way to attain the joy that is rightfully yours? By giving Christ what is rightfully His: your heart, your soul, and your life.

Dear Lord, You have given me so many reasons to celebrate. Today, I choose an attitude of cheerfulness. Let me be a joyful Christian, Lord, quick to smile and slow to anger. And, I will share Your goodness with all whom I meet so that Your love might shine in me and through me. Amen

CHRIST'S LOVE

I am the good shepherd. The good shepherd lays down his life for the sheep.

John 10:11 HCSB

But God proves His own love for us in that while we were still sinners Christ died for us!

Romans 5:8 HCSB

No one has greater love than this, that someone would lay down his life for his friends.

John 15:13 HCSB

Who can separate us from the love of Christ? Can affliction or anguish or persecution or famine or nakedness or danger or sword? . . . No, in all these things we are more than victorious through Him who loved us.

Romans 8:35, 37 HCSB

Just as the Father has loved Me, I also have loved you. Remain in My love.

John 15:9 HCSB

Christ proved His love for you and me on the cross at Calvary. Even though we are imperfect, fallible human beings, and, even though we have, on countless occasions, fallen short of God's commandments, Christ loves us still. His love is perfect and unchanging; it does not waver and it does not pass away. In return, we are called to be steadfast in our love for Him.

As we accept Christ's love and honor His commandments, our lives bear testimony to His power and to His grace. Christ's love changes everything. May we accept it and share it, today, tomorrow, and forever.

No man ever loved like Jesus. He taught the blind to see and the dumb to speak. He died on the cross to save us. He bore our sins. And now God says, "Because He did, I can forgive you."

Billy Graham

Dear Lord, I offer thanksgiving and praise for the gift of Your only begotten Son. His love is boundless, infinite, and eternal. And, as an expression of my love for Him, let me share His message with my family, with my friends, and with the world. Amen

CONFIDENCE

So I strive always to keep my conscience clear before God and man.

Acts 24:16 NIV

If then you were raised with Christ, seek those things which are above, where Christ is, sitting at the right hand of God. Set your mind on things above, not on things on the earth.

Colossians 3:1-2 NKJV

Let us come near to God with a sincere heart and a sure faith, because we have been made free from a guilty conscience, and our bodies have been washed with pure water.

Hebrews 10:22 NCV

I will maintain my righteousness and never let go of it; my conscience will not reproach me as long as I live.

Job 27:6 NIV

For indeed, the kingdom of God is within you.

Luke 17:21 NKJV

Are you a confident believer, or do you live under a cloud of uncertainty and doubt? As a Christian, you have many reasons to be confident. After all, God is in His heaven; Christ has risen; and you are the recipient of God's grace. Despite these blessings, you may, from time to time, find yourself being tormented by negative emotions—and you are certainly not alone.

But even when you feel very distant from God, remember that God is never distant from you. When you sincerely seek His presence, He will touch your heart, calm your fears, and restore your confidence.

God never leaves your side, not for an instant. He is always with you, always willing to calm the storms of life. When you sincerely seek His presence—and when you genuinely seek to establish a deeper, more meaningful relationship with His Son—God is prepared to touch your heart, to calm your fears, to answer your doubts, and to restore your confidence.

Dear Lord, give me confidence and courage for the coming day. When I am fearful, let me feel Your strength. Let me always trust in Your promises, Lord, and let me draw strength from those promises and from Your unending love. Amen

CONSCIENCE

Now the goal of our instruction is love from a pure heart, a good conscience, and a sincere faith.

1 Timothy 1:5 HCSB

If then you were raised with Christ, seek those things which are above, where Christ is, sitting at the right hand of God. Set your mind on things above, not on things on the earth.

Colossians 3:1-2 NKJV

And do not be conformed to this world, but be transformed by the renewing of your mind, that you may prove what is that good and acceptable and perfect will of God.

Romans 12:2 NKJV

For indeed, the kingdom of God is within you.

Luke 17:21 NKJV

I always do my best to have a clear conscience toward God and men.

Acts 24:16 HCSB

Billy Graham correctly observed, "Most of us follow our conscience as we follow a wheelbarrow. We push it in front of us in the direction we want to go." To do so, of course, is a profound mistake. Yet all of us, on occasion, have failed to listen to the voice that God planted in our hearts, and all of us have suffered the consequences.

God gave you a conscience for a very good reason: to make your path conform to His will. Wise believers make it a practice to listen carefully to that quiet internal voice. Count yourself among that number. When your conscience speaks, listen and learn. In all likelihood, God is trying to get His message through. And in all likelihood, it is a message that you desperately need to hear.

To go against one's conscience is neither safe nor right. Here I stand. I cannot do otherwise.

Martin Luther

Dear Lord, You speak to me through the gift of Your Holy Word. And, Father, You speak to me through that still small voice that tells me right from wrong. Let me follow Your way, Lord, and, in these quiet moments, show me Your plan for this day, that I might serve You. Amen

COURAGE

The LORD himself goes before you and will be with you; he will never leave you nor forsake you. Do not be afraid; do not be discouraged.

Deuteronomy 31:8 NIV

So do not fear, for I am with you; do not be dismayed, for I am your God. I will strengthen you and help you; I will uphold you with my righteous right hand.

Isaiah 41:10 NIV

Peace I leave with you, my peace I give unto you: not as the world giveth, give I unto you. Let not your heart be troubled, neither let it be afraid.

John 14:27 KJV

In thee, O Lord, do I put my trust; let me never be put into confusion.

Psalm 71:1 KJV

I can do everything through him that gives me strength.

Philippians 4:13 NIV

Life can be difficult and discouraging at times. During our darkest moments, God offers us strength and courage if we turn our hearts and our prayers to Him.

As believing Christians, we have every reason to live courageously. After all, the ultimate battle has already been fought and won on the cross at Calvary. But sometimes, because we are imperfect human beings who possess imperfect faith, we fall prey to fear and doubt. The answer to our fears, of course, is God.

The next time you find your courage tested to the limit, remember that God is as near as your next breath. He is your shield and your strength; He is your protector and your deliverer. Call upon Him in your hour of need and then be comforted. Whatever your challenge, whatever your trouble, God can handle it . . . and will!

Lord, sometimes I face challenges that leave me breathless. When I am fearful, let me lean upon You. Keep me ever mindful, Lord, that You are my God, my strength, and my shield. With You by my side, I have nothing to fear. And, with Your Son Jesus as my Savior, I have received the priceless gift of eternal life. Help me to be a grateful and courageous servant this day and every day. Amen

DECISIONS

If you don't know what you're doing, pray to the Father. He loves to help. You'll get his help, and won't be condescended to when you ask for it. Ask boldly, believingly, without a second thought. People who "worry their prayers" are like wind-whipped waves. Don't think you're going to get anything from the Master that way, adrift at sea, keeping all your options open.

James 1:5-8 MSG

But Daniel purposed in his heart that he would not defile himself . . . .

Daniel 1:8 KJV

I am offering you life or death, blessings or curses. Now, choose life! . . . To choose life is to love the Lord your God, obey him, and stay close to him.

Deuteronomy 30:19-20 NCV

The thing you should want most is God's kingdom and doing what God wants. Then all these other things you need will be given to you.

Matthew 6:33 NCV

From the instant you wake in the morning until the moment you nod off to sleep at night, you have the opportunity to make countless decisions: decisions about the things you do, decisions about the words you speak, and decisions about the thoughts you choose to think. Simply put, the quality of those decisions determines, to a surprising extent, the quality of your life.

Some decisions are easy to make because the consequences of those decisions are small. When the person behind the counter asks, "Want fries with that?" the necessary response requires little thought because the aftermath of that decision is relatively unimportant.

People who can never quite make up their minds usually make themselves miserable. So when in doubt, be decisive. It's the decent way to live.

As we trust God to give us wisdom for today's decisions, He will lead us a step at a time into what He wants us to be doing in the future.

Theodore Epp

Dear Lord, help me to make decisions that are pleasing to You. Help me be honest, patient, and kind. And help me to follow the teachings of Jesus, not just today, but every day. Amen

DISAPPOINTMENTS

We are hard pressed on every side, yet not crushed; we are perplexed, but not in despair.

2 Corinthians 4:8 NKJV

Sometimes I ask God, my rock-solid God, "Why did you let me down? Why am I walking around in tears, harassed by enemies?"

Psalm 42:9 MSG

When you go through deep waters and great trouble, I will be with you. When you go through the rivers of difficulty, you will not drown! When you walk through the fire of oppression, you will not be burned up; the flames will not consume you. For I am the Lord, your God . . . .

Isaiah 43:2-3 NLT

Is anyone among you suffering? Then he must pray.

James 5:13 NASB

These things I have spoken to you, that in Me you may have peace. In the world you will have tribulation; but be of good cheer, I have overcome the world.

John 16:33 NKJV

No life plan is perfect; sometimes, we must make major modifications in our hopes, dreams, goals, and plans . . . or else.

Some of our most important dreams are the ones we abandon. Some of our most important goals are the ones we don't attain. Sometimes, our most important journeys are the ones that we take to the winding conclusion of what seem to be dead end streets. Thankfully, with God there are no dead ends; there are only opportunities to learn, to yield, to trust, to serve, and to grow.

The next time you experience one of life's inevitable disappointments, don't despair and don't be afraid to try "Plan B." Consider every setback an opportunity to choose a different, more appropriate path. Have faith that God may indeed be leading you in an entirely different direction, a direction of His choosing. And as you take your next step, remember that what looks like a dead end to you may, in fact, be the fast lane according to God.

———

Dear Lord, when I face the inevitable disappointments of life, remind me that You are in control. You are the Giver of all good things, Father, and You will bless me today, tomorrow, and forever. Amen

DISCIPLESHIP

Be imitators of God, therefore, as dearly loved children.

Ephesians 5:1 NIV

Don't work hard only when your master is watching and then shirk when he isn't looking; work hard and with gladness all the time, as though working for Christ, doing the will of God with all your hearts.

Ephesians 6:6-7 TLB

And Jesus said unto them, Come ye after me, and I will make you to become fishers of men. And straightway they forsook their nets, and followed him.

Mark 1:17-18 KJV

He has showed you, O man, what is good. And what does the LORD require of you? To act justly and to love mercy and to walk humbly with your God.

Micah 6:8 NIV

If your life honors the name of Jesus, he will honor you.

2 Thessalonians 1:12 MSG

When Jesus addressed His disciples, He warned that each one must "take up his cross and follow me." The disciples must have known exactly what the Master meant. In Jesus' day, prisoners were forced to carry their own crosses to the location where they would be put to death. Thus, Christ's message was clear: in order to follow Him, Christ's disciples must deny themselves and, instead, trust Him completely. Nothing has changed since then.

If we are to be disciples of Christ, we must trust Him and place Him at the very center of our beings. Jesus never comes "next." He is always first. The paradox, of course, is that only by sacrificing ourselves to Him do we gain salvation for ourselves.

Do you seek to be a worthy disciple of Christ? Then pick up His cross today and every day that you live. When you do, He will bless you now and forever.

Dear Jesus, because I am Your disciple, I will trust You, I will obey Your teachings, and I will share Your Good News. You have given me life abundant and life eternal, and I will follow You today and forever. Amen

DISCIPLINE

No discipline seems enjoyable at the time, but painful. Later on, however, it yields the fruit of peace and righteousness to those who have been trained by it.

Hebrews 12:11 HCSB

The one who follows instruction is on the path to life, but the one who rejects correction goes astray.

Proverbs 10:17 HCSB

For this very reason, make every effort to supplement your faith with goodness, goodness with knowledge, knowledge with self-control, self-control with endurance, endurance with godliness.

2 Peter 1:5-6 HCSB

I discipline my body and bring it under strict control, so that after preaching to others, I myself will not be disqualified.

1 Corinthians 9:27 HCSB

Therefore by their fruits you will know them.

Matthew 7:20 NKJV

Wise men teach their families the importance of discipline using both words and examples. Disciplined men understand that God doesn't reward laziness or misbehavior. To the contrary, God expects His believers to lead lives that are above reproach. And, He punishes those who disobey His commandments.

In Proverbs 28:19, God's message is clear: "He who works his land will have abundant food, but the one who chases fantasies will have his fill of poverty" (NIV). When we work diligently and consistently, we can expect a bountiful harvest. But we must never expect the harvest to precede the labor. First, we must lead lives of discipline and obedience; then, we will reap the never-ending rewards that God has promised.

If one examines the secret behind a championship football team, a magnificent orchestra, or a successful business, the principal ingredient is invariably discipline.

James Dobson

Lord, I want to be a disciplined believer. Let me use my time wisely, and let me teach others by the faithfulness of my conduct, today and every day. Amen

DOUBTS

If you don't know what you're doing, pray to the Father. He loves to help. You'll get his help, and won't be condescended to when you ask for it. Ask boldly, believingly, without a second thought. People who "worry their prayers" are like wind-whipped waves. Don't think you're going to get anything from the Master that way, adrift at sea, keeping all your options open.

James 1:5-8 MSG

Purify your hearts, ye double-minded.

James 4:8 KJV

Immediately the father of the child cried out and said with tears, "Lord, I believe; help my unbelief!"

Mark 9:24 NKJV

So He said, "Come." And when Peter had come down out of the boat, he walked on the water to go to Jesus. But when he saw that the wind was boisterous, he was afraid; and beginning to sink he cried out, saying, "Lord, save me!" And immediately Jesus stretched out His hand and caught him, and said to him, "O you of little faith, why did you doubt?" And when they got into the boat, the wind ceased.

Matthew 14:29-32 NKJV

I f you've never had any doubts about your faith, then you can stop reading this page now and skip to the next page. But if you've ever been plagued by doubts about your faith or your God, keep reading.

Even some of the most faithful Christians are, at times, beset by occasional bouts of discouragement and doubt. But even when we feel far removed from God, God is never far removed from us. He is always with us, always willing to calm the storms of life—always willing to replace our doubts with comfort and assurance.

Whenever you're plagued by doubts, that's precisely the moment you should seek God's presence by genuinely seeking to establish a deeper, more meaningful relationship with His Son. Then you may rest assured that in time, God will calm your fears, answer your prayers, and restore your confidence.

———

Dear God, sometimes this world can be a puzzling place, filled with uncertainty and doubt. When I am unsure of my next step, keep me mindful that You are always near and that You can overcome any challenge. Give me faith, Father, and let me remember always that with Your love and Your power, I can live courageously and faithfully today and every day. Amen

DREAMS

Live full lives, full in the fullness of God. God can do anything, you know—far more than you could ever imagine or guess or request in your wildest dreams! He does it not by pushing us around but by working within us, his Spirit deeply and gently within us.

Ephesians 3:19-20 MSG

I came so they can have real and eternal life, more and better life than they ever dreamed of.

John 10:10 MSG

It is pleasant to see dreams come true, but fools will not turn from evil to attain them.

Proverbs 13:19 NLT

Where there is no vision, the people perish . . . .

Proverbs 29:18 KJV

Be of good courage, and he shall strengthen your heart, all ye that hope in the LORD.

Psalm 31:24 KJV

Do you expect your future to be bright? Are you willing to dream king-sized dreams . . . and are you willing to work diligently to make those dreams happen? Hopefully so—after all, God promises that we can do "all things" through Him. Yet most of us, even the most devout among us, live far below our potential. We take half measures; we dream small dreams; we waste precious time and energy on the distractions of the world. But God has other plans for us.

Our Creator intends that we live faithfully, hopefully, courageously, and abundantly. He knows that we are capable of so much more; and He wants us to do the things we're capable of doing; and He wants us to begin doing those things today.

The biggest human temptation is to settle for too little.

Thomas Merton

Dear Lord, give me the courage to dream and the faithfulness to trust in Your perfect plan. When I am worried or weary, give me strength for today and hope for tomorrow. Keep me mindful of Your healing power, Your infinite love, and Your eternal salvation. Amen

ENCOURAGEMENT

Let's see how inventive we can be in encouraging love and helping out, not avoiding worshipping together as some do but spurring each other on.

Hebrews 10:24-25 MSG

Watch the way you talk. Let nothing foul or dirty come out of your mouth. Say only what helps, each word a gift.

Ephesians 4:29 MSG

Encourage each other. Live in harmony and peace. Then the God of love and peace will be with you.

2 Corinthians 13:11 NLT

Let the word of Christ dwell in you richly in all wisdom; teaching and admonishing one another in psalms and hymns and spiritual songs, singing with grace in your hearts to the Lord.

Colossians 3:16 KJV

But encourage one another day after day, as long as it is still called "Today," so that none of you will be hardened by the deceitfulness of sin.

Hebrews 3:13 NASB

Barnabas, a man whose name meant "Son of Encouragement," was a leader in the early Christian church. He was known for his kindness and for his ability to encourage others. Because of Barnabas, many people were introduced to Christ. And today, as believers living in a difficult world, we must seek to imitate the "Son of Encouragement."

We imitate Barnabas when we speak kind words to our families and to our friends. We imitate Barnabas when our actions give credence to our beliefs. We imitate Barnabas when we are generous with our possessions and with our praise. We imitate Barnabas when we give hope to the hopeless and encouragement to the downtrodden.

Today, be like Barnabas: become a source of encouragement to those who cross your path. When you do so, you will quite literally change the world, one person—and one moment—at a time.

———

Dear Lord, let me celebrate the accomplishments of others. Make me a source of genuine, lasting encouragement to my family and friends. And let my words and deeds be worthy of Your Son, the One who gives me strength and salvation, this day and for all eternity. Amen

ENTHUSIASM

Whatever you do, do it enthusiastically, as something done for the Lord and not for men.

Colossians 3:23 HCSB

Never be lazy in your work, but serve the Lord enthusiastically.

Romans 12:11 NLT

Whatever work you do, do your best, because you are going to the grave, where there is no working . . . .

Ecclesiastes 9:10 NCV

I have seen that there is nothing better than for a person to enjoy his activities, because that is his reward. For who can enable him to see what will happen after he dies?

Ecclesiastes 3:22 HCSB

Do your work with enthusiasm. Work as if you were serving the Lord, not as if you were serving only men and women.

Ephesians 6:7 NCV

A re you "burning" with enthusiasm about your life, your friends, your family, and your future? If so, congratulations, and keep up the good work! But, if your spiritual batteries are running low, perhaps you're spending too much energy focusing on your losses and too little time planning for future victories.

Writer Sara Jordan has this simple (but effective) advice: "Every day give yourself a good mental shampoo."

So if you're feeling tired or troubled, or both, don't despair. Instead, take time to count your blessings as you focus on things positive. And while you're at it, seek strength from the Source that never fails. When you sincerely petition God, He will give you all the strength you need to live victoriously through Him.

Diligence applies to whatever you do in your Christian life. Anything done in the Lord's service is worth doing with enthusiasm and care.

John MacArthur

Dear Lord, if the obligations of the day leave me exhausted or discouraged, I will turn to You for strength and for renewal. When I follow Your will for my life, You will renew my enthusiasm. Let Your will be my will, Lord, and let me find strength and courage in You. Amen

ETERNAL LIFE

And this is the testimony: God has given us eternal life, and this life is in His Son. The one who has the Son has life. The one who doesn't have the Son of God does not have life.

1 John 5:11-12 HCSB

I have written these things to you who believe in the name of the Son of God, so that you may know that you have eternal life.

1 John 5:13 HCSB

Jesus said to her, "I am the resurrection and the life. The one who believes in Me, even if he dies, will live. Everyone who lives and believes in Me will never die—ever. Do you believe this?"

John 11:25-26 HCSB

Pursue righteousness, godliness, faith, love, endurance, and gentleness. Fight the good fight for the faith; take hold of eternal life, to which you were called and have made a good confession before many witnesses.

1 Timothy 6:11-12 HCSB

Your ability to envision the future, like your life here on earth, is limited. God's vision, however, is not burdened by any such limitations. He sees all things, He knows all things, and His plans for you endure for all time.

God's plans are not limited to the events of life-here-on-earth. Your Heavenly Father has bigger things in mind for you . . . much bigger things. So praise the Creator for the gift of eternal life and share the Good News with all who cross your path. You have given your heart to the Son, so you belong to the Father—today, tomorrow, and for all eternity.

———

Teach us to set our hopes on heaven, to hold firmly to the promise of eternal life, so that we can withstand the struggles and storms of this world.

Max Lucado

———

Lord, You have given me the priceless gift of eternal life through Your Son Jesus. Keep the hope of heaven fresh in my heart. While I am in this world, help me to pass through it with faith in my heart and praise on my lips for You. Amen

EXAMPLE

You should be an example to the believers in speech, in conduct, in love, in faith, in purity.

1 Timothy 4:12 HCSB

Do everything without grumbling and arguing, so that you may be blameless and pure.

Philippians 2:14–15 HCSB

Set an example of good works yourself, with integrity and dignity in your teaching.

Titus 2:7 HCSB

For the kingdom of God is not in talk but in power.

1 Corinthians 4:20 HCSB

Therefore since we also have such a large cloud of witnesses surrounding us, let us lay aside every weight and the sin that so easily ensnares us, and run with endurance the race that lies before us.

Hebrews 12:1 HCSB

Okay, here's a question: What kind of example are you? Are you the kind of guy whose life serves as a powerful example of decency and morality? Are you a guy whose behavior serves as a positive role model for others? Are you the kind of guy whose actions, day in and day out, are based upon integrity, fidelity, and a love for the Lord? If so, you are not only blessed by God, you are also a powerful force for good in a world that desperately needs positive influences such as yours.

Phillips Brooks advised, "Be such a man, and live such a life, that if every man were such as you, and every life a life like yours, this earth would be God's Paradise." And that's sound advice because our families and friends are watching . . . and so, for that matter, is God.

———

Men are mirrors, or "carriers" of Christ to other men. Sometimes unconscious carriers.

C. S. Lewis

———

Lord, make me a worthy example to my family and friends. And, let my words and my deeds serve as a testimony to the changes You have made in my life. Let me praise You, Father, by following in the footsteps of Your Son, and let others see Him through me. Amen

God's Promises About . . .

FAILURE

If we confess our sins to him, he is faithful and just to forgive us
and to cleanse us from every wrong.

1 John 1:9 NLT

If you hide your sins, you will not succeed. If you confess and reject
them, you will receive mercy.

Proverbs 28:13 NCV

If you listen to constructive criticism, you will be at home among
the wise.

Proverbs 15:31 NLT

So we're not giving up. How could we! Even though on the outside
it often looks like things are falling apart on us, on the inside, where
God is making new life, not a day goes by without his unfolding
grace.

2 Corinthians 4:16 MSG

I waited patiently for the LORD; he turned to me and heard my cry.
He lifted me out of the slimy pit, out of the mud and mire; he set
my feet on a rock and gave me a firm place to stand. He put a new
song in my mouth, a hymn of praise to our God . . . .

Psalm 40:1-3 NIV

The occasional disappointments and failures of life are inevitable. Such setbacks are simply the price that we must occasionally pay for our willingness to take risks as we follow our dreams. But even when we encounter bitter disappointments, we must never lose faith.

The reassuring words of Hebrews 10:36 remind us that when we persevere, we will eventually receive that which God has promised. What's required is perseverance, not perfection.

When we encounter the inevitable difficulties of life here on earth, God stands ready to protect us. Our responsibility, of course, is to ask Him for protection. When we call upon Him in heartfelt prayer, He will answer—in His own time and according to His own plan—and He will heal us. And, while we are waiting for God's plans to unfold and for His healing touch to restore us, we can be comforted in the knowledge that our Creator can overcome any obstacle, even if we cannot.

———

Dear Lord, when I encounter failures and disappointments, keep me mindful that You are in control. Let me persevere— even if my soul is troubled—and let me follow Your Son Jesus Christ this day and forever. Amen

FAITH

Now faith is the reality of what is hoped for, the proof of what is not seen.

Hebrews 11:1 HCSB

Now without faith it is impossible to please God, for the one who draws near to Him must believe that He exists and rewards those who seek Him.

Hebrews 11:6 HCSB

For we walk by faith, not by sight.

2 Corinthians 5:7 HCSB

If you do not stand firm in your faith, then you will not stand at all.

Isaiah 7:9 HCSB

Jesus said, "Because you have seen Me, you have believed. Blessed are those who believe without seeing."

John 20:29 HCSB

The first element of a successful life is faith: faith in God, faith in His Son, and faith in His promises. If we place our lives in God's hands, our faith is rewarded in ways that we—as human beings with clouded vision and limited understanding—can scarcely comprehend. But, if we seek to rely solely upon our own resources, or if we seek earthly success outside the boundaries of God's commandments, we reap a bitter harvest for ourselves and for our loved ones.

Do you desire the abundance and success that God has promised? Then trust Him today and every day that you live. Trust Him with every aspect of your life. Trust His promises, and trust in the saving grace of His only begotten Son. Then, when you have entrusted your future to the Giver of all things good, rest assured that your future is secure, not only for today, but also for all eternity.

Faith is not anti-intellectual. It is an act of man that reaches beyond the limits of our five senses.

Billy Graham

Heavenly Father, help me to be a man of faith. Help me to remember that You are always near and that You can overcome any challenge. With Your love and Your power, Lord, I can live courageously and faithfully today and every day. Amen

FAMILY

You must choose for yourselves today whom you will serve . . . as for me and my family, we will serve the Lord.

Joshua 24:15 NCV

Love must be without hypocrisy. Detest evil; cling to what is good. Show family affection to one another with brotherly love. Outdo one another in showing honor.

Romans 12:9–10 HCSB

Their first responsibility is to show godliness at home and repay their parents by taking care of them. This is something that pleases God very much.

1 Timothy 5:4 NLT

Every kingdom divided against itself will be ruined, and every city or household divided against itself will not stand.

Matthew 12:25 NIV

Let love and faithfulness never leave you . . . write them on the tablet of your heart.

Proverbs 3:3 NIV

The words of 1 Timothy 5:8 are unambiguous: if God has blessed us with families, then He expects us to care for them. Sometimes, this profound responsibility seems daunting. And sometimes, even for the most dedicated Christian men, family life holds moments of frustration and disappointment. But, for those who are lucky enough to live in the presence of a close-knit, caring clan, the rewards far outweigh the demands.

No family is perfect, and neither is yours. Despite the inevitable challenges of providing for your family, and despite the occasional hurt feelings of family life, your clan is God's gift to you. Give thanks to the Giver for the gift of family . . . and act accordingly.

———

The God who adopted you into His forever family knows how to make earthly families work.

Charles Stanley

———

Dear Lord, I am part of Your family, and I praise You for Your gifts and for Your love. You have also blessed me with my earthly family, and I pray for them, that they might be protected and blessed by You. Let me show love and acceptance for my family, Lord, so that through me, they might come to know and to love You. Amen

FEAR

Even when I go through the darkest valley, I fear no danger, for You are with me.

Psalm 23:4 HCSB

Don't be afraid. Only believe.

Mark 5:36 HCSB

For I, the Lord your God, hold your right hand and say to you: Do not fear, I will help you.

Isaiah 41:13 HCSB

I sought the Lord, and He heard me, and delivered me from all my fears.

Psalm 34:4 NKJV

Do not fear, for I am with you; do not be afraid, for I am your God. I will strengthen you; I will help you; I will hold on to you with My righteous right hand.

Isaiah 41:10 HCSB

A frightening storm rose quickly on the Sea of Galilee, and the disciples were afraid. Because of their limited faith, they feared for their lives. When they turned to Jesus, He calmed the waters and He rebuked His disciples for their lack of faith in Him.

On occasion, we, like the disciples, are frightened by the inevitable storms of life. Why are we afraid? Because we, like the disciples, possess imperfect faith.

When we genuinely accept God's promises as absolute truth, when we trust Him with life here on earth and life eternal, we have little to fear. Faith in God is the antidote to worry. Faith in God is the foundation of courage and the source of power. Today, let us trust God more completely and, by doing so, move beyond our fears to a place of abundance, assurance, and peace.

Your Word reminds me, Lord, that even when I walk through the valley of the shadow of death, I need fear no evil, for You are with me, and You comfort me. Thank You, Lord, for a perfect love that casts out fear. Let me live courageously and faithfully this day and every day. Amen

God's Promises About . . .

FEAR OF GOD

Honor all people. Love the brotherhood. Fear God. Honor the king.

1 Peter 2:17 NKJV

Fear the LORD your God, serve him only and take your oaths in his name.

Deuteronomy 6:13 NIV

The fear of the Lord is the beginning of knowledge, but fools despise wisdom and discipline.

Proverbs 1:7 NIV

The fear of the Lord is a fountain of life . . . .

Proverbs 14:27 NIV

How blessed is everyone who fears the LORD, who walks in His ways.

Psalm 128:1 NASB

God's hand shapes the universe, and it shapes our lives. God maintains absolute sovereignty over His creation, and His power is beyond comprehension. As believers, we must cultivate a sincere respect for God's awesome power. God has dominion over all things, and until we acknowledge His sovereignty, we lack the humility we need to live righteously, and we lack the humility we need to become wise.

The fear of the Lord is, indeed, the beginning of knowledge. So today, as you face the realities of everyday life, remember this: until you acquire a healthy, respectful fear of God's power, your education is incomplete, and so is your faith.

The fear of God is the death of every other fear.

C. H. Spurgeon

Dear Lord, let my greatest fear be the fear of displeasing You. I will strive, Father, to obey Your commandments and seek Your will this day and every day of my life. Amen

God's Promises About . . .

FELLOWSHIP

You must get along with each other. You must learn to be considerate of one another, cultivating a life in common.

1 Corinthians 1:10 MSG

Don't you realize that all of you together are the temple of God and that the Spirit of God lives in you?

1 Corinthians 3:16 NLT

Don't become partners with those who reject God. How can you make a partnership out of right and wrong? That's not partnership; that's war. Is light best friends with dark?

2 Corinthians 6:14 MSG

He keeps us in step with each other. His very breath and blood flow through us, nourishing us so that we will grow up healthy in God, robust in love.

Ephesians 4:16 MSG

You can develop a healthy, robust community that lives right with God and enjoy its results only if you do the hard work of getting along with each other, treating each other with dignity and honor.

James 3:18 MSG

I t is almost impossible to underestimate the importance of Christian fellowship. When you join with fellow believers in worship and praise, you enrich their lives in the same way that they enrich yours.

Christ promised that wherever two or more are gathered together in His name, He is there also (Matthew 18:20). So let us gather together in the presence of Christ and worship Him with thanksgiving in our hearts, praise on our lips, and fellow believers by our sides.

———————

Christian brotherhood is not an ideal which we must realize; it is rather a reality created by God in Christ in which we may participate.

Dietrich Bonhoeffer

———————

Heavenly Father, You have given me a community of supporters called the church. Let our fellowship be a reflection of the love we feel for each other and the love we feel for You. Amen

God's Promises About . . .

FOLLOWING CHRIST

Then he told them what they could expect for themselves: "Anyone who intends to come with me has to let me lead."

Luke 9:23 MSG

I've laid down a pattern for you. What I've done, you do.

John 13:15 MSG

No one can serve two masters. Either he will hate the one and love the other, or he will be devoted to the one and despise the other.

Matthew 6:24 NIV

Whoever is not willing to carry the cross and follow me is not worthy of me. Those who try to hold on to their lives will give up true life. Those who give up their lives for me will hold on to true life.

Matthew 10:38-39 NCV

If anyone would come after me, he must deny himself and take up his cross and follow me.

Mark 8:34 NIV

When we have been saved by Christ, we can, if we choose, become passive Christians. We can sit back, secure in our own salvation, and let other believers spread the healing message of Jesus. But to do so is wrong. Instead, we are commanded to become disciples of the One who has saved us, and to do otherwise is a sin of omission with terrible consequences.

God's Word reminds us again and again that our Savior intends that we pick up His cross and follow Him. Are you willing to walk in the footsteps of the One from Galilee? Jesus wants your attention and your devotion. And He deserves them both now.

———————

Christ is to be sought and bought with any pains, at any price; we cannot buy this gold too dear. He is a jewel worth more than a thousand worlds. Get him, and get all; miss him and miss all.

Thomas Brooks

———————

Dear Lord, You sent Jesus to save the world and to save me. I thank You for Jesus, and I will do my best to follow Him, today and forever. Amen

FORGIVENESS

All bitterness, anger and wrath, insult and slander must be removed from you, along with all wickedness. And be kind and compassionate to one another, forgiving one another, just as God also forgave you in Christ.

Ephesians 4:31-32 HCSB

See to it that no one repays evil for evil to anyone, but always pursue what is good for one another and for all.

1 Thessalonians 5:15 HCSB

A person's insight gives him patience, and his virtue is to overlook an offense.

Proverbs 19:11 HCSB

And forgive us our sins, for we ourselves also forgive everyone in debt to us.

Luke 11:4 HCSB

Be merciful, just as your Father also is merciful.

Luke 6:36 HCSB

Forgiveness is a choice. We can either choose to forgive those who have injured us, or not. When we follow God's teachings by offering forgiveness to His children, we are blessed. But when we allow bitterness and resentment to poison our hearts, we are tortured by our own shortsightedness.

Do you harbor resentment against anyone? If so, you are faced with an important decision: whether or not to forgive the person who has hurt you. God's instructions are clear: He wants you to forgive. Period.

To forgive or not to forgive: that is the question. The answer should be obvious. The time to forgive is now . . . always now.

—————

Forgiving is a gift God has given us for healing ourselves before we are ready to help anyone else.

Dr. Lewis Smedes

—————

Heavenly Father, give me a forgiving heart. When I am bitter, Your Word reminds me that forgiveness is Your commandment. Let me be Your obedient servant, Lord, and let me be a man who forgives others just as You have forgiven me. Amen

FUTURE

What a God we have! And how fortunate we are to have him, this Father of our Master Jesus! Because Jesus was raised from the dead, we've been given a brand-new life and have everything to live for, including a future in heaven—and the future starts now!

1 Peter 1:3-4 MSG

"I say this because I know what I am planning for you," says the Lord. "I have good plans for you, not plans to hurt you. I will give you hope and a good future."

Jeremiah 29:11 NCV

Wisdom is pleasing to you. If you find it, you have hope for the future.

Proverbs 24:14 NCV

When troubles come and all these awful things happen to you, in future days you will come back to God, your God, and listen obediently to what he says. God, your God, is above all a compassionate God. In the end he will not abandon you, he won't bring you to ruin, he won't forget the covenant with your ancestors which he swore to them.

Deuteronomy 4:30-31 MSG

L et's talk for a minute about the future . . . your future. How bright do you believe your future to be? Well, if you're a faithful believer, God has plans for you that are so bright that you'd better pack several pairs of sunglasses and a lifetime supply of sunblock!

The way that you think about your future will play a powerful role in determining how things turn out (it's called the "self-fulfilling prophecy," and it applies to everybody, including you). So here's another question: Are you expecting a terrific tomorrow, or are you dreading a terrible one? The answer to that question will have a powerful impact on the way tomorrow unfolds.

Today, as you live in the present and look to the future, remember that God has an amazing plan for you. Act—and believe—accordingly. And one more thing: don't forget the sunblock.

Hoping for a good future without investing in today is like a farmer waiting for a crop without ever planting any seed.

John Maxwell

Dear Lord, as I look to the future, I will place my trust in You. If I become discouraged, I will turn to You. If I am afraid, I will seek strength in You. You are my Father, and I will place my hope, my trust, and my faith in You. Amen

GENEROSITY

So let him give; not grudgingly, or of necessity: for God loveth a cheerful giver.

2 Corinthians 9:7 KJV

Above all, love each other deeply, because love covers a multitude of sins.

1 Peter 4:8 NIV

The man with two tunics should share with him who has none, and the one who has food should do the same.

Luke 3:11 NIV

I tell you the truth, whatever you did for one of the least of these brothers of mine, you did for me.

Matthew 25:40 NIV

The good person is generous and lends lavishly . . . .

Psalm 112:5 MSG

God's gifts are beyond description, His blessings are beyond comprehension. God has been incredibly generous with us, and He rightfully expects us to be generous with others. That's why the thread of generosity is woven into the very fabric of God's teachings.

In the Old Testament, we are told that, "The good person is generous and lends lavishly . . . ." (Psalm 112:5 MSG). And in the New Testament we are instructed, "Freely you have received, freely give" (Matthew 10:8 NKJV). These principles still apply. As we establish priorities for our days and our lives, we are advised to give freely of our time, our possessions, and our love—just as God has given freely to us.

Of course, we can never fully repay God for His gifts, but we can share them with others. And we should.

If you desire to become a more generous person, don't wait for your income to change. Change your heart.

John Maxwell

Lord, make me a generous and cheerful giver. Help me to give generously of my time and my possessions as I care for those in need. And, make me a humble giver, Lord, so that all the glory and the praise might be Yours. Amen

GIFTS

Do not neglect the gift that is in you.

1 Timothy 4:14 HCSB

Every generous act and every perfect gift is from above, coming down from the Father of lights.

James 1:17 HCSB

I remind you to keep ablaze the gift of God that is in you.

2 Timothy 1:6 HCSB

According to the grace given to us, we have different gifts: If prophecy, use it according to the standard of faith; if service, in service; if teaching, in teaching; if exhorting, in exhortation; giving, with generosity; leading, with diligence; showing mercy, with cheerfulness.

Romans 12:6-8 HCSB

Based on the gift they have received, everyone should use it to serve others, as good managers of the varied grace of God.

1 Peter 4:10 HCSB

A ll men possess special gifts—bestowed from the Father above—and you are no exception. But, your gift is no guarantee of success; it must be cultivated and nurtured; otherwise, it will go unused . . . and God's gift to you will be squandered.

Today, make a promise to yourself that you will earnestly seek to discover the talents that God has given you. Then, nourish those talents and make them grow. Finally, vow to share your gifts with the world for as long as God gives you the power to do so. After all, the best way to say "Thank You" for God's gifts is to use them.

―――――

God is still in the process of dispensing gifts, and He uses ordinary individuals like us to develop those gifts in other people.

Howard Hendricks

―――――

Lord, I praise You for Your priceless gifts. I give thanks for Your creation, for Your Son, and for the unique talents and opportunities that You have given me. Let me use my gifts for the glory of Your kingdom, this day and every day. Amen

GOD'S FORGIVENESS

Praise be to the God and Father of our Lord Jesus Christ! In his great mercy he has given us new birth into a living hope through the resurrection of Jesus Christ from the dead.

1 Peter 1:3 NIV

But God's mercy is great, and he loved us very much. Though we were spiritually dead because of the things we did against God, he gave us new life with Christ. You have been saved by God's grace.

Ephesians 2:4-5 NCV

And the LORD said, "I will cause all my goodness to pass in front of you, and I will proclaim my name, the LORD, in your presence. I will have mercy on whom I will have mercy, and I will have compassion on whom I will have compassion.

Exodus 33:19 NIV

So let us come boldly to the throne of our gracious God. There we will receive his mercy, and we will find grace to help us when we need it.

Hebrews 4:16 NLT

The Bible promises you this: When you ask God for forgiveness, He will give it. No questions asked; no explanations required.

God's power to forgive, like His love, is infinite. Despite your shortcomings, despite your sins, God offers you immediate forgiveness. It's time to take Him up on His offer.

When it comes to forgiveness, God doesn't play favorites and neither should you. You should forgive all the people who have harmed you (not just the people who have asked for forgiveness or the ones who have made restitution). Complete forgiveness is God's way, and it should be your way, too. Anything less is not enough.

Every time we forgive others, deserving it or not, we have a reminder of God's forgiveness.

Franklin Graham

Dear Lord, when I ask for forgiveness, You give it. Thank You, Father, for forgiving me when I make mistakes. Today, I will be quick to forgive others, just as You have forgiven me. Amen

GOD'S LOVE

Unfailing love surrounds those who trust the LORD.

Psalm 32:10 NLT

For the LORD your God has arrived to live among you. He is a mighty savior. He will rejoice over you with great gladness. With his love, he will calm all your fears. He will exult over you by singing a happy song.

Zephaniah 3:17 NLT

But God demonstrates His own love toward us, in that while we were still sinners, Christ died for us.

Romans 5:8 NKJV

For he chose us in him before the creation of the world to be holy and blameless in his sight. In love he predestined us to be adopted as his sons through Jesus Christ, in accordance with his pleasure and will . . . .

Ephesians 1:4-5 NIV

For God so loved the world that he gave his only Son, so that everyone who believes in him will not perish but have eternal life.

John 3:16 NLT

Where can we find God's love? Everywhere. God's love transcends space and time. It reaches beyond the heavens, and it touches the darkest, smallest corner of every human heart. When we sincerely open our minds and hearts to God, His love does not arrive "some day"—it arrives immediately.

Joyce Meyer reminds us that, "God has the marvelous ability to love us in the midst of our imperfections." And if He can love us unconditionally, we should find the wisdom and the courage to love ourselves, come what may.

So today, take God at His word and welcome His love into your heart. When you do, God's transcendent love will surround you and transform you, now and always.

The love of God is one of the great realities of the universe, a pillar upon which the hope of the world rests. But it is a personal, intimate thing too. God does not love populations. He loves people. He loves not masses, but men.

A. W. Tozer

Thank You, dear God, for Your love. You are my loving Father. I thank You for Your love and for Your Son. I will praise You; I will worship You; and, I will love You today, tomorrow, and forever. Amen

GOD'S PLAN

"I say this because I know what I am planning for you," says the Lord. "I have good plans for you, not plans to hurt you. I will give you hope and a good future."

Jeremiah 29:11 NCV

People may make plans in their minds, but the Lord decides what they will do.

Proverbs 16:9 NCV

There is no wisdom, no insight, no plan that can succeed against the Lord.

Proverbs 21:30 NIV

Unless the Lord builds a house, the work of the builders is useless.

Psalm 127:1 NLT

The Lord says, "I will guide you along the best pathway for your life. I will advise you and watch over you."

Psalm 32:8 NLT

God has plans for your life, but He won't force those plans upon you. To the contrary, He has given you free will, the ability to make decisions on your own. With that freedom to choose comes the responsibility of living with the consequences of the choices you make.

If you seek to live in accordance with God's will for your life—and you should—then you will live in accordance with His commandments. You will study God's Word, and you will be watchful for His signs. You will associate with fellow Christians who will encourage your spiritual growth, and you will listen to that inner voice that speaks to you in the quiet moments of your daily devotionals.

God intends to use you in wonderful, unexpected ways if you let Him. The decision to seek God's plan and to follow it is yours and yours alone. The consequences of that decision have implications that are both profound and eternal, so choose carefully.

———————

Lord, You have a plan for my life. Let me discover it and live it. Today, I will seek Your will, knowing that when I trust in You, dear Father, I am eternally blessed. Amen

GOD'S POWER

For His divine power has given us everything required for life and godliness, through the knowledge of Him who called us by His own glory and goodness.

2 Peter 1:3 HCSB

For the LORD your God is God of gods and Lord of lords, the great God, mighty and awesome.

Deuteronomy 10:17 NIV

I pray also that you will have greater understanding in your heart so you will know the hope to which he has called us and that you will know how rich and glorious are the blessings God has promised his holy people. And you will know that God's power is very great for us who believe.

Ephesians 1:18-19 NCV

Proclaim the power of God, whose majesty is over Israel, whose power is in the skies. You are awesome, O God, in your sanctuary; the God of Israel gives power and strength to his people. Praise be to God!

Psalm 68:34-35 NIV

Because God's power is limitless, it is far beyond the comprehension of mortal minds. But even though we cannot fully understand the awesome heart of God, we can praise it, worship it, and marvel at its mercy.

God's ability to love is not burdened by boundaries or by limitations. The love that flows from the awesome heart of God is infinite—and today presents yet another opportunity to celebrate His love.

When we worship God with faith and assurance, when we place Him at the absolute center of our lives, we invite His love into our hearts. In turn, we grow to love Him more deeply as we sense His love for us. St. Augustine wrote, "I love you, Lord, not doubtingly, but with absolute certainty. Your Word beat upon my heart until I fell in love with you, and now the universe and everything in it tells me to love you." Let us pray that we, too, will turn our hearts to the Creator, knowing with certainty that His awesome heart has ample room for each of us, and that we, in turn, must make room in our hearts for Him.

———

Heavenly Father, You are all-knowing and all-powerful. Today, I praise You for Your love, and I marvel at the glory of Your Creation. With You as my protector, Lord, I am secure, today and forever. Amen

GOD'S PRESENCE

Come near to God, and God will come near to you. You sinners, clean sin out of your lives. You who are trying to follow God and the world at the same time, make your thinking pure.

James 4:8 NCV

Again, this is God's command: to believe in his personally named Son, Jesus Christ. He told us to love each other, in line with the original command. As we keep his commands, we live deeply and surely in him, and he lives in us. And this is how we experience his deep and abiding presence in us: by the Spirit he gave us.

1 John 3:23-24 MSG

For the eyes of the Lord range throughout the earth to strengthen those whose hearts are fully committed to him.

2 Chronicles 16:9 NIV

God did this so that men would seek him and perhaps reach out for him and find him, though he is not far from each one of us.

Acts 17:27 NIV

If God is everywhere, why does He sometimes seem so far away? The answer to that question, of course, has nothing to do with God and everything to do with us.

When we begin each day on our knees, in praise and worship to Him, God often seems very near indeed. But, if we ignore God's presence or—worse yet—rebel against it altogether, the world in which we live becomes a spiritual wasteland.

Are you tired, discouraged, or fearful? Be comforted because God is with you. Are you confused? Listen to the quiet voice of your Heavenly Father. Are you bitter? Talk with God and seek His guidance. Are you celebrating a great victory? Thank God and praise Him. He is the Giver of all things good.

In whatever condition you find yourself, wherever you are—whether you are happy or sad, victorious or vanquished, troubled or triumphant—celebrate God's presence. And be comforted. God is not just near. He is here.

———

Dear Lord, You are with me when I am strong and when I am weak. You never leave my side, even when it seems to me that You are far away. Today and every day, let me trust Your promises and let me feel Your love. Amen

GOD'S PROTECTION

Finally, my brethren, be strong in the Lord and in the power of His might. Put on the whole armor of God, that you may be able to stand against the wiles of the devil.

Ephesians 6:10-11 NKJV

The Lord your God in your midst, The Mighty One, will save; He will rejoice over you with gladness, He will quiet you with His love, He will rejoice over you with singing.

Zephaniah 3:17 NKJV

God is my shield, saving those whose hearts are true and right.

Psalm 7:10 NLT

Those who trust the Lord are like Mount Zion, which sits unmoved forever. As the mountains surround Jerusalem, the Lord surrounds his people now and forever.

Psalm 125:1-2 NCV

But the Lord will be a refuge for His people.

Joel 3:16 HCSB

The hand of God encircles us and comforts us in times of adversity. In times of hardship, He restores our strength; in times of sorrow, He dries our tears. When we are troubled or weak or embittered, God is as near as our next breath.

God has promised to protect us, and He intends to fulfill His promise. In a world filled with dangers and temptations, God is the ultimate armor. In a world filled with misleading messages, God's Word is the ultimate truth. In a world filled with more frustrations than we can count, God's Son offers the ultimate peace.

Will you accept God's peace and wear God's armor against the dangers of our world? Hopefully so, because when you do, you can live courageously, knowing that you possess the ultimate protection: God's unfailing love for you.

Under heaven's lock and key, we are protected by the most efficient security system available: the power of God.

Charles Swindoll

Lord, You are my Shepherd. You care for me; You comfort me; You watch over me; and You have saved me. I will praise You, Father, for Your glorious works, for Your protection, for Your love, and for Your Son. Amen

GOD'S TIMING

He [Jesus] said to them: "It is not for you to know the times or dates the Father has set by his own authority."

Acts 1:7 NIV

He has made everything beautiful in its time. He has also set eternity in the hearts of men; yet they cannot fathom what God has done from beginning to end.

Ecclesiastes 3:11 NIV

Yet the LORD longs to be gracious to you; he rises to show you compassion. For the LORD is a God of justice. Blessed are all who wait for him!

Isaiah 30:18 NIV

I wait for the LORD, my soul waits, and in his word I put my hope.

Psalm 130:5 NIV

I waited patiently for the LORD; and He inclined to me, and heard my cry.

Psalm 40:1 NKJV

Sometimes, the hardest thing to do is to wait. This is especially true when we're in a hurry and when we want things to happen now, if not sooner! But God's plan does not always happen in the way that we would like or at the time of our own choosing. Our task—as believing Christians who trust in a benevolent, all knowing Father—is to wait patiently for God to reveal Himself.

We human beings are, by nature, impatient. We know what we want, and we know exactly when we want it: RIGHT NOW! But, God knows better. He has created a world that unfolds according to His own timetable, not ours . . . thank goodness!

———

God does not promise to keep us out of the storms and floods, but He does promise to sustain us in the storm, and then bring us out in due time for His glory when the storm has done its work.

Warren Wiersbe

———

Dear Lord, Your wisdom is infinite, and the timing of Your heavenly plan is perfect. You have a plan for my life that is grander than I can imagine. When I am impatient, remind me that You are never early or late. You are always on time, Father, so let me trust in You. Amen

God's Promises About . . .

GRATITUDE

Everything created by God is good, and nothing is to be rejected, if it is received with gratitude; for it is sanctified by means of the word of God and prayer.

1 Timothy 4:4-5 NASB

As you therefore have received Christ Jesus the Lord, so walk in Him, having been firmly rooted and now being built up in Him and established in your faith, just as you were instructed, and overflowing with gratitude.

Colossians 2:6-7 NASB

Therefore, since we receive a kingdom which cannot be shaken, let us show gratitude, by which we may offer to God an acceptable service with reverence and awe . . . .

Hebrews 12:28 NASB

I will praise the name of God with a song, and will magnify him with thanksgiving.

Psalm 69:30 KJV

It is good to give thanks to the Lord, to sing praises to the Most High. It is good to proclaim your unfailing love in the morning, your faithfulness in the evening.

Psalm 92:1-2 NLT

For most of us, life is busy and complicated. We have countless responsibilities, some of which begin before sunrise and many of which end long after sunset. Amid the rush and crush of the daily grind, it is easy to lose sight of God and His blessings. But, when we forget to slow down and say "Thank You" to our Maker, we rob ourselves of His presence, His peace, and His joy.

Our task, as believing Christians, is to praise God many times each day. Then, with gratitude in our hearts, we can face our daily duties with the perspective and power that only He can provide.

Contentment comes when we develop an attitude of gratitude for the important things we do have in our lives that we tend to take for granted if we have our eyes staring longingly at our neighbor's stuff.

Dave Ramsey

Lord, make me a man with a grateful heart. You have given me much; when I think of Your grace and goodness, I am humbled and thankful. Today, let me praise You not just through my words but also through my deeds . . . and may all the glory be Yours. Amen

HAPPINESS

How happy are those whose way is blameless, who live according to the law of the Lord! Happy are those who keep His decrees and seek Him with all their heart.

Psalm 119:1-2 HCSB

If they serve Him obediently, they will end their days in prosperity and their years in happiness.

Job 36:11 HCSB

The one who understands a matter finds success, and the one who trusts in the Lord will be happy.

Proverbs 16:20 HCSB

Happy are the people whose strength is in You, whose hearts are set on pilgrimage.

Psalm 84:5 HCSB

A joyful heart is good medicine, but a broken spirit dries up the bones.

Proverbs 17:22 HCSB

Happiness depends less upon our circumstances than upon our thoughts. When we turn our thoughts to God, to His gifts, and to His glorious creation, we experience the joy that God intends for His children. But, when we focus on the negative aspects of life, we suffer needlessly.

Do you sincerely want to be a happy Christian? Then set your mind and your heart upon God's love and His grace. The fullness of life in Christ is available to all who seek it and claim it. Count yourself among that number. Seek first the salvation that is available through a personal relationship with Jesus Christ, and then claim the joy, the peace, and the spiritual abundance that the Shepherd offers His sheep.

Christianity says we were created by a righteous God to flourish and be exhilarated in a righteous environment. God has "wired" us in such a way that the more righteous we are, the more we'll actually enjoy life.

Abraham Lincoln

Dear Lord, You are my strength and my joy. I will rejoice in the day that You have made, and I will give thanks for the countless blessings that You have given me. Let me be a joyful Christian, Father, as I share the Good News of Your Son, and let me praise You for all the marvelous things You have done. Amen

God's Promises About . . .

HELPING OTHERS

When we have the opportunity to help anyone, we should do it. But we should give special attention to those who are in the family of believers.

Galatians 6:10 NCV

You address me as "Teacher" and "Master," and rightly so. That is what I am. So if I, the Master and Teacher, washed your feet, you must now wash each other's feet. I've laid down a pattern for you. What I've done, you do.

John 13:15 MSG

The one who blesses others is abundantly blessed; those who help others are helped.

Proverbs 11:25 MSG

Whenever you are able, do good to people who need help.

Proverbs 3:27 NCV

Sometimes we would like to help make the world a better place, but we're not sure how to do it. Jesus told the story of the "Good Samaritan," a man who helped a fellow traveler when no one else would. We, too, should be good Samaritans when we find people who need our help. A good place to start helping other people is at home. And of course, we should also offer our help at school and at church.

Another way that we can help other people is to pray for them. God always hears our prayers, so we should talk with Him as often as we can. When we do, we're not only doing a wonderful thing for the people we pray for, we're also doing a wonderful thing for ourselves, too. Why? Because we feel better about ourselves when we're helping other people. And the more we help others, the better we should feel about ourselves.

Do all the good you can. By all the means you can. In all the ways you can. In all the places you can. At all the times you can. To all the people you can. As long as ever you can.

John Wesley

Dear Lord, let me help others in every way that I can. Jesus served others; I can too. I will serve other people with my good deeds and with my prayers, and I will give thanks for all those who serve and protect our nation and our world. Amen

HOLINESS

Real wisdom, God's wisdom, begins with a holy life and is characterized by getting along with others. It is gentle and reasonable, overflowing with mercy and blessings, not hot one day and cold the next, not two-faced.

James 3:17 MSG

Pursue peace with all people, and holiness, without which no one will see the Lord.

Hebrews 12:14 NKJV

Since everything here today might well be gone tomorrow, do you see how essential it is to live a holy life?

2 Peter 3:11 MSG

But now you must be holy in everything you do, just as God—who chose you to be his children—is holy. For he himself has said, "You must be holy because I am holy."

1 Peter 1:15-16 NLT

You will teach me how to live a holy life. Being with you will fill me with joy; at your right hand I will find pleasure forever.

Psalm 16:11 NCV

A life of righteousness is lived in accordance with God's commandments. A righteous man strives to be faithful, honest, generous, disciplined, loving, kind, humble, and grateful, to name only a few of the more obvious qualities which are described in God's Word.

If we seek to follow the steps of Jesus, we must seek to live according to His teachings. In short, we must, to the best of our abilities, live according to the principles contained in the Holy Bible. When we do, we become powerful examples to our families and friends of the blessings that God bestows upon righteous men.

The destined end of man is not happiness nor health, but holiness. God's one aim is the production of saints. He is not an eternal blessing machine for men; he did not come to save men out of pity; he came to save men because he had created them to be holy.

Oswald Chambers

Holy, Holy, Holy . . . You are a righteous and holy God who commands that I seek to be holy and righteous. Forgive me when I fall short, Lord, and renew a right spirit within me. Let me serve You and obey the teachings of Your Word. Lead me far from temptation, Father, and guide me in Your will for my life. Amen

HONESTY

As we have received mercy, we faint not; but have renounced the hidden things of dishonesty, not walking in craftiness, nor handling the word of God deceitfully; but, by manifestation of the truth, commending ourselves to every man's conscience in the sight of God.

2 Corinthians 4:1-2 KJV

Therefore laying aside falsehood, speak truth, each one of you, with his neighbor, for we are members of one another.

Ephesians 4:25 NASB

But when he, the Spirit of truth, comes, he will guide you into all truth . . . .

John 16:13 NIV

Jesus answered, "I am the way and the truth and the life. No one comes to the Father except through me."

John 14:6 NIV

And ye shall know the truth, and the truth shall make you free.

John 8:32 KJV

It has been said on many occasions and in many ways that honesty is the best policy. For believers, it is far more important to note that honesty is God's policy. And if we are to be servants worthy of Jesus Christ, we must be honest and forthright in our communications with others. Sometimes, honesty is difficult; sometimes, honesty is painful; sometimes, honesty is inconvenient; but always honesty is God's commandment.

In the Book of Proverbs, we read, "The Lord detests lying lips, but he delights in men who are truthful" (12:22 NIV). Clearly, we must strive to be men whose words are pleasing to our Creator. Truth is God's way, and it must be our way, too, even when telling the truth is difficult. As Christian men, we can do no less.

A lie is like a snowball: the further you roll it, the bigger it becomes.

Martin Luther

Dear Lord, You command Your children to walk in truth. Let me follow Your commandment. Give me the courage to speak honestly, and let me walk righteously with You so that others might see Your eternal truth reflected in my words and my deeds. Amen

God's Promises About . . .

HOPE

Be of good courage, and he shall strengthen your heart, all ye that hope in the LORD.

Psalm 31:24 KJV

Be joyful in hope, patient in affliction, faithful in prayer.

Romans 12:12 NIV

The Lord is good to those whose hope is in him, to the one who seeks him; it is good to wait quietly for the salvation of the Lord.

Lamentations 3:25-26 NIV

Blessed is he whose help is the God of Jacob, whose hope is in the LORD his God, the Maker of heaven and earth, the sea, and everything in them—the LORD, who remains faithful forever.

Psalm 146:5-6 NIV

May the God of hope fill you with all joy and peace as you trust in him, so that you may overflow with hope by the power of the Holy Spirit.

Romans 15:13 NIV

There are few sadder sights on earth than the sight of a person who has lost all hope. In difficult times, hope can be elusive, but Christians need never lose it. After all, God is good; His love endures; He has promised His children the gift of eternal life.

If you find yourself falling into the spiritual traps of worry and discouragement, consider the words of Jesus. It was Christ who promised, "In the world you will have tribulation; but be of good cheer, I have overcome the world" (John 16:33 NKJV). This world is, indeed, a place of trials and tribulations, but as believers, we are secure. God has promised us peace, joy, and eternal life. And, of course, God always keeps His promises.

And because we know Christ is alive, we have hope for the present and hope for life beyond the grave.

Billy Graham

Dear Lord, make me a man of hope. If I become discouraged, let me turn to You. If I grow weary, let me seek strength in You. When I face adversity, let me seek Your will and trust Your Word. In every aspect of my life, I will trust You, Father, so that my heart will be filled with faith and hope, this day and forever. Amen

God's Promises About . . .

HUMILITY

Clothe yourselves with humility toward one another, because God resists the proud, but gives grace to the humble.

1 Peter 5:5 HCSB

Humble yourselves therefore under the mighty hand of God, so that He may exalt you in due time, casting all your care upon Him, because He cares about you.

1 Peter 5:6-7 HCSB

But He said to me, "My grace is sufficient for you, for power is perfected in weakness." Therefore, I will most gladly boast all the more about my weaknesses, so that Christ's power may reside in me.

2 Corinthians 12:9 HCSB

If My people who are called by My name will humble themselves, and pray and seek My face, and turn from their wicked ways, then I will hear from heaven, and will forgive their sin and heal their land.

2 Chronicles 7:14 NKJV

God's Word clearly instructs us to be humble. And that's good because, as fallible human beings, we have so very much to be humble about! Yet some of us continue to puff ourselves up, seeming to say, "Look at me!" To do so is wrong.

As Christians, we have been refashioned and saved by Jesus Christ, and that salvation came not because of our own good works but because of God's grace. How, then, can we be prideful? The answer, of course, is that, if we are honest with ourselves and with our God, we simply can't be boastful . . . we must, instead, be eternally grateful and exceedingly humble. The good things in our lives, including our loved ones, come from God. He deserves the credit—and we deserve the glorious experience of giving it to Him.

Jesus had a humble heart. If He abides in us, pride will never dominate our lives.

Billy Graham

Lord, make me a man with a humble heart. Keep me mindful, dear God, that all my gifts come from You. When I feel prideful, remind me that You sent Your Son to be a humble carpenter and that Jesus was ridiculed on a cross. Let me grow beyond my need for earthly praise, Lord, and when I seek approval, let me look only to You. Amen

God's Promises About . . .

INTEGRITY

Till I die, I will not deny my integrity. I will maintain my righteousness and never let go of it; my conscience will not reproach me as long as I live.

Job 27:5-6 NIV

May integrity and uprightness protect me, because my hope is in you.

Psalm 25:21 NIV

In everything set them an example by doing what is good. In your teaching show integrity, seriousness and soundness of speech that cannot be condemned, so that those who oppose you may be ashamed because they have nothing bad to say about us.

Titus 2:7 NIV

A good name is to be chosen rather than great riches, loving favor rather than silver and gold.

Proverbs 22:1 NKJV

The integrity of the upright shall guide them . . . .

Proverbs 11:3 KJV

Charles Swindoll correctly observed, "Nothing speaks louder or more powerfully than a life of integrity." Godly men and women agree.

Integrity is built slowly over a lifetime. It is a precious thing—difficult to build but easy to tear down. As believers in Christ, we must seek to live each day with discipline, honesty, and faith. When we do, at least two things happen: integrity becomes a habit, and God blesses us because of our obedience to Him.

Living a life of integrity isn't always the easiest way, but it is always the right way. And God clearly intends that it should be our way, too.

Integrity is not a given factor in everyone's life. It is a result of self-discipline, inner trust, and a decision to be relentlessly honest in all situations in our lives.

John Maxwell

Dear Lord, You search my heart and know me far better than I know myself. May I be Your worthy servant, and may I live according to Your commandments. Let me be a man of integrity, Lord, and let my words and deeds be a testimony to You, today and always. Amen

God's Promises About . . .

JESUS

The next day John saw Jesus coming toward him and said, "Here is the Lamb of God, who takes away the sin of the world!"

John 1:29 HCSB

I am the door. If anyone enters by Me, he will be saved.

John 10:9 NKJV

I have come as a light into the world, so that everyone who believes in Me would not remain in darkness.

John 12:46 HCSB

I am the true vine, and My Father is the vineyard keeper. Every branch in Me that does not produce fruit He removes, and He prunes every branch that produces fruit so that it will produce more fruit.

John 15:1-2 HCSB

But we do see Jesus—made lower than the angels for a short time so that by God's grace He might taste death for everyone—crowned with glory and honor because of the suffering of death.

Hebrews 2:9 HCSB

Our circumstances change but Jesus does not. Even when the world seems to be trembling beneath our feet, Jesus remains the spiritual bedrock that cannot be moved.

The old familiar hymn begins, "What a friend we have in Jesus . . . ." No truer words were ever penned. Jesus is the sovereign friend and ultimate Savior of mankind. Christ showed enduring love for His believers by willingly sacrificing His own life so that we might have eternal life. Let us love Him, praise Him, and share His message of salvation with our neighbors and with the world.

Jesus is the personal approach from the unseen God coming so near that he becomes inescapable. You don't have to find him—you just have to consent to be found.

E. Stanley Jones

Dear Lord, You sent Your Son to die on a cross so that I might have eternal life. And because Jesus was a man who walked this earth, You possess a perfect understanding of all humanity, including my own frailties and shortcomings. I praise You, Lord, for Your love, for Your forgiveness, for Your grace, and for Your Son. Let me share the Good News of Jesus Christ, the One who became a man so that I might become His, not only for today, but also for all eternity. Amen

JOY

Rejoice, and be exceeding glad: for great is your reward in heaven . . . .

Matthew 5:12 KJV

Thou wilt show me the path of life: in thy presence is fulness of joy; at thy right hand there are pleasures for evermore.

Psalm 16:11 KJV

Weeping may endure for a night, but joy cometh in the morning.

Psalm 30:5 KJV

I will thank you, Lord, with all my heart; I will tell of all the marvelous things you have done. I will be filled with joy because of you. I will sing praises to your name, O Most High.

Psalm 9:1-2 NLT

Delight thyself also in the LORD; and he shall give thee the desires of thine heart.

Psalm 37:4 KJV

Are you a man whose joy is evident for all to see? If so, congratulations: you're doing God's will. Psalm 100 reminds us that, as believers, we have every reason to celebrate: "Shout for joy to the Lord, all the earth. Worship the Lord with gladness" (vv. 1-2 NIV). Yet sometimes, amid the inevitable hustle and bustle of life here on earth, we can forfeit—albeit temporarily—the joy that God intends for our lives.

If you find yourself feeling discouraged or worse, it's time to slow down and have a quiet conversation with your Creator. If your heart is heavy, open the door of your soul to the Father and to His only begotten Son. Christ offers you His peace and His joy. Accept it and share it freely, just as Christ has freely shared His joy with you.

Dear Lord, You have given me so many blessings; let me celebrate Your gifts. Make me thankful, loving, responsible, and wise. I praise You, Father, for the gift of Your Son and for the priceless gift of salvation. Make me be a joyful Christian, a worthy example to others, and a dutiful servant to You this day and forever. Amen

God's Promises About . . .

KINDNESS

Finally, all of you be of one mind, having compassion for one another; love as brothers, be tenderhearted, be courteous.

1 Peter 3:8 NKJV

Love is patient; love is kind.

1 Corinthians 13:4 HCSB

And may the Lord make you increase and abound in love to one another and to all.

1 Thessalonians 3:12 NKJV

And be kind and compassionate to one another, forgiving one another, just as God also forgave you in Christ.

Ephesians 4:32 HCSB

Pure and undefiled religion before our God and Father is this: to look after orphans and widows in their distress and to keep oneself unstained by the world.

James 1:27 HCSB

The instructions of Colossians 3:12 are unambiguous: as Christians, we are to be compassionate, humble, gentle, and kind. But sometimes, we fall short. In the busyness and confusion of daily life, we may neglect to share a kind word or a kind deed. This oversight hurts others, but it hurts us most of all.

Today, slow yourself down and be alert for those who need your smile, your kind words, or your helping hand. Make kindness a centerpiece of your dealings with others. They will be blessed, and you will be too. Today, honor Christ by following His Golden Rule. He expects no less, and He deserves no less.

Heavenly Father, sometimes this world can become a demanding place, a place where I rush through the day with my eyes focused only on my next step. Slow me down, Lord, and give me wisdom and peace so that I might look beyond my own needs and see the needs of those around me. Today, help me to be generous, compassionate, and understanding. Today, let me spread kind words and deeds to all who cross my path. Today, let the love for Christ shine through me. And let me show kindness to all who need the healing touch of our Master's hand. Amen

LIFE

Watch your life and doctrine closely. Persevere in them, because if you do, you will save both yourself and your hearers.

1 Timothy 4:16 NIV

His divine power has given us everything we need for life and godliness through our knowledge of him who called us by his own glory and goodness.

2 Peter 1:3 NIV

Seek the Lord, and ye shall live . . . .

Amos 5:6 KJV

I urge you to live a life worthy of the calling you have received.

Ephesians 4:1 NIV

And Jesus said unto them, I am the bread of life: he that cometh to me shall never hunger; and he that believeth on me shall never thirst.

John 6:35 KJV

L ife is a glorious gift from God. Treat it that way. This day, like every other, is filled to the brim with opportunities, challenges, and choices. But, no choice that you make is more important than the choice you make concerning God. Today, you will either place Him at the center of your life—or not—and the consequences of that choice have implications that are both temporal and eternal.

Sometimes, we don't intentionally neglect God; we simply allow ourselves to become overwhelmed with the demands of everyday life. And then, without our even realizing it, we gradually drift away from the One we need most. Thankfully, God never drifts away from us. He remains always present, always steadfast, always loving.

As you begin this day, place God and His Son where they belong: in your head, in your prayers, on your lips, and in your heart. And then, with God as your guide and companion, let the journey begin . . .

Lord, You are the Giver of all life, and You created me to have fellowship with You. Let me live a life that pleases You, Lord, and let me thank You always for Your blessings. You love me and protect me, Heavenly Father. Let me be grateful, and let me live for You today and throughout eternity. Amen

LOVE

Though I speak with the tongues of men and of angels, but have not love, I have become sounding brass or a clanging cymbal.

1 Corinthians 13:1 NKJV

Beloved, if God so loved us, we also ought to love one another.

1 John 4:11 NASB

Love one another deeply, from the heart.

1 Peter 1:22 NIV

Above all, love each other deeply, because love covers over a multitude of sins.

1 Peter 4:8 NIV

May the Lord cause you to increase and abound in love for one another, and for all people.

1 Thessalonians 3:12 NASB

L ove, like everything else in this wonderful world, begins and ends with God, but the middle part belongs to us. During the brief time that we have here on earth, God has given each of us the opportunity to become a loving person—or not. God has given each of us the opportunity to be kind, to be courteous, to be cooperative, and to be forgiving—or not. God has given each of us the chance to obey the Golden Rule, or to make up our own rules as we go. If we obey God's rules, we're safe, but if we do otherwise, we're headed for trouble and fast.

Here in the real world, the choices that we make have consequences. The decisions that we make and the results of those decisions determine the quality of our relationships. It's as simple as that.

Suppose that I understand the Bible. And, suppose that I am the greatest preacher who ever lived! The Apostle Paul wrote that unless I have love, "I am nothing."

Billy Graham

Lord, love is Your commandment. Help me always to remember that the gift of love is a precious gift indeed. Let me nurture love and treasure it. And, keep me mindful that the essence of love is not to receive it, but to give it, today and forever. Amen

LOVING GOD

We love him, because he first loved us.

1 John 4:19 KJV

This is love: not that we loved God, but that he loved us and sent his Son as an atoning sacrifice for our sins.

1 John 4:10 NIV

Love the LORD your God with all your heart and with all your soul and with all your strength.

Deuteronomy 6:5 NIV

I will sing of the LORD'S great love forever; with my mouth I will make your faithfulness known through all generations.

Psalm 89:1 NIV

And we know that in all things God works for the good of those who love him, who have been called according to his purpose.

Romans 8:28 NIV

If you want to know God in a more meaningful way, you'll need to open up your heart and let Him in. C. S. Lewis observed, "A person's spiritual health is exactly proportional to his love for God." If you hope to receive a full measure of God's spiritual blessings, you must invite your Creator to rule over your heart. When you honor God in this way, His love expands to fill your heart and bless your life.

St. Augustine wrote, "I love you, Lord, not doubtingly, but with absolute certainty. Your Word beat upon my heart until I fell in love with you, and now the universe and everything in it tells me to love you."

Today, open your heart to the Father. And let your obedience be a fitting response to His never-ending love.

———————

God has a genuine, passionate affection for each of us and invites us to open our hearts to that love and then return love to Him with deep sincerity.

Bill Hybels

———————

Dear Lord, You have blessed me with a love that is infinite and eternal. Make me Your loving servant, today and throughout eternity. And, let me show my love for You by sharing Your message and Your love with my family, with my friends, and with the world. Amen

MATERIALISM

For where your treasure is, there your heart will be also.

Luke 12:34 NKJV

He who trusts in his riches will fall, but the righteous will flourish . . . .

Proverbs 11:28 NKJV

No one can serve two masters. The person will hate one master and love the other, or will follow one master and refuse to follow the other. You cannot serve both God and worldly riches.

Matthew 6:24 NCV

A man's life does not consist in the abundance of his possessions.

Luke 12:15 NIV

Yes, a person is a fool to store up earthly wealth but not have a rich relationship with God.

Luke 12:21 NLT

D o you sometimes feel swamped by your possessions? Do you seem to spend more and more time keeping track of the things you own while making mental notes of the things you intend to buy? If so, here's a word of warning: your fondness for material possessions is getting in the way of your relationships—your relationships with the people around you and your relationship with God.

Society teaches us to honor possessions . . . God teaches us to honor people. And if we seek to be worthy followers of Christ, we must never invest too much energy in the acquisition of "stuff." Earthly riches are here today and all too soon gone. Our real riches, of course, are in heaven, and that's where we should focus our thoughts and our energy.

———

There is absolutely no evidence that complexity and materialism lead to happiness. On the contrary, there is plenty of evidence that simplicity and spirituality lead to joy, a blessedness that is better than happiness.

Dennis Swanberg

———

Heavenly Father, when I focus intently upon You, I am blessed. When I focus too intently on the acquisition of material possessions, I am troubled. Make my priorities pleasing to You, Father, and make me a worthy servant of Your Son. Amen

God's Promises About . . .

MIRACLES

Looking at them, Jesus said, "With men it is impossible, but not with God, because all things are possible with God."

Mark 10:27 HCSB

I assure you: The one who believes in Me will also do the works that I do. And he will do even greater works than these, because I am going to the Father.

John 14:12 HCSB

But as it is written: "Eye has not seen, nor ear heard, nor have entered into the heart of man the things which God has prepared for those who love Him."

1 Corinthians 2:9 NKJV

For nothing will be impossible with God.

Luke 1:37 HCSB

You are the God who works wonders; You revealed Your strength among the peoples.

Psalm 77:14 HCSB

Do you believe in an all-powerful God who can do miraculous things in you and through you? You should. But perhaps, as you have faced the inevitable struggles of life-here-on-earth, you have—without realizing it—placed limitations on God. To do so is a profound mistake. God's power has no such limitations, and He can work mighty miracles in your own life if you let Him.

Do you lack a firm faith in God's power to perform miracles for you and your loved ones? If so, you are attempting to place limitations on a God who has none. Instead of doubting your Heavenly Father, you must place yourself in His hands. Instead of doubting God's power, you must trust it. Expect Him to work miracles, and be watchful. With God, absolutely nothing is impossible, including an amazing assortment of miracles that He stands ready, willing, and perfectly able to perform for you and yours.

Dear Lord, absolutely nothing is impossible for You. Let me trust in Your power and in Your miracles. When I lose hope, give me faith; when others lose hope, let me tell them of Your glorious works. Today, Lord, keep me mindful that You are a God of infinite possibilities and infinite love. Amen

MISSIONS

But you will receive power when the Holy Spirit has come upon you, and you will be My witnesses in Jerusalem, in all Judea and Samaria, and to the ends of the earth.

Acts 1:8 HCSB

After this the Lord appointed 70 others, and He sent them ahead of Him in pairs to every town and place where He Himself was about to go. He told them: "The harvest is abundant, but the workers are few. Therefore, pray to the Lord of the harvest to send out workers into His harvest. Now go; I'm sending you out like lambs among wolves."

Luke 10:1-3 HCSB

Then He said to them, "Go into all the world and preach the gospel to the whole creation."

Mark 16:15 HCSB

What I tell you in the dark, speak in the light. What you hear in a whisper, proclaim on the housetops.

Matthew 10:27 HCSB

The Good News of Jesus Christ should be shouted from the rooftops by believers the world over. But all too often, it is not. For a variety of reasons, many Christians keep their beliefs to themselves, and when they do, the world suffers because of their failure to speak up.

As believers, we are called to share the transforming message of Jesus with our families, with our neighbors, and with the world. Jesus commands us to become fishers of men. And, the time to go fishing is now. We must share the Good News of Jesus Christ today—tomorrow may indeed be too late.

The glory of God, and, as our only means of glorifying Him, the salvation of human souls, is the real business of life.

C. S. Lewis

Lord, even if I never leave home, make me a missionary for You. Let me share the Good News of Your Son, and let me tell of Your love and of Your grace. Make me a faithful servant for You, Father, now and forever. Amen

God's Promises About . . .

OBEDIENCE

Therefore, get your minds ready for action, being self-disciplined, and set your hope completely on the grace to be brought to you at the revelation of Jesus Christ. As obedient children, do not be conformed to the desires of your former ignorance but, as the One who called you is holy, you also are to be holy in all your conduct.

1 Peter 1:13-15 HCSB

Now by this we know that we know Him, if we keep His commandments.

1 John 2:3 NKJV

But whoever keeps His word, truly the love of God is perfected in him. By this we know that we are in Him. He who says he abides in Him ought himself also to walk just as He walked.

1 John 2:5-6 NKJV

For this is what love for God is: to keep His commands. Now His commands are not a burden, because whatever has been born of God conquers the world. This is the victory that has conquered the world: our faith.

1 John 5:3-4 HCSB

God's laws are eternal and unchanging: obedience leads to abundance and joy; disobedience leads to disaster. God has given us a guidebook for righteous living called the Holy Bible. If we trust God's Word and live by it, we are blessed. But, if we choose to ignore God's commandments, the results are as predictable as they are tragic.

Life is a series of decisions and choices. Each day, we make countless decisions that can bring us closer to God . . . or not. When we live according to God's commandments, we earn for ourselves the abundance and peace that He intends for our lives.

Do you seek God's peace and His blessings? Then obey Him. When you're faced with a difficult choice or a powerful temptation, seek God's counsel and trust the counsel He gives. Invite God into your heart and live according to His commandments. When you do, you will be blessed today, and tomorrow, and forever.

Dear Lord, when I am tempted to disobey Your commandments, correct my errors and guide my path. Make me a faithful steward of my talents, my opportunities, and my possessions so that Your kingdom may be glorified, now and forever. Amen

God's Promises About . . .

OPPORTUNITIES

Make the most of every opportunity.

Colossians 4:5 NIV

Let us not lose heart in doing good, for in due time we shall reap if we do not grow weary. So then, while we have opportunity, let us do good to all men, and especially to those who are of the household of the faith.

Galatians 6:9-10 NASB

Dear brothers and sisters, whenever trouble comes your way, let it be an opportunity for joy. For when your faith is tested, your endurance has a chance to grow. So let it grow, for when your endurance is fully developed, you will be strong in character and ready for anything.

James 1:2-4 NLT

Remember ye not the former things, neither consider the things of old. Behold, I will do a new thing . . . .

Isaiah 43:18-19 KJV

Are you excited about the opportunities of today and thrilled by the possibilities of tomorrow? Do you confidently expect God to lead you to a place of abundance, peace, and joy? Hopefully so. After all, you are surrounded by countless opportunities to improve your own life and the lives of those you love.

Today, as you prepare to meet the duties of everyday life, pause and consider your opportunities. And then think for a moment about your potential to make the world a better place for you and your loved ones.

You can do many things to make your life—and your world—a happier, kinder, gentler place. And that's precisely what God wants you to do . . . starting now.

He who waits until circumstances completely favor his undertaking will never accomplish anything.

Martin Luther

Lord, as I take the next steps on my life's journey, let me take them with You. Whatever this day may bring, I thank You for the opportunity to live abundantly. Let me lean upon You, Father—and trust You—this day and forever. Amen

OPTIMISM

The Lord is my light and my salvation; whom shall I fear? The Lord is the strength of my life; of whom shall I be afraid?

Psalm 27:1 KJV

Make me to hear joy and gladness . . . .

Psalm 51:8 KJV

I can do everything through him that gives me strength.

Philippians 4:13 NIV

Be of good courage, and he shall strengthen your heart, all ye that hope in the LORD.

Psalm 31:24 KJV

Finally, brethren, whatsoever things are true, whatsoever things are honest, whatsoever things are just, whatsoever things are pure, whatsoever things are lovely, whatsoever things are of good report; if there be any virtue, and if there be any praise, think on these things.

Philippians 4:8 KJV

Christians have every reason to be optimistic about life. As John Calvin observed, "There is not one blade of grass, there is no color in this world that is not intended to make us rejoice." But, sometimes, rejoicing is the last thing on our minds. Sometimes, we fall prey to worry, frustration, anxiety, or sheer exhaustion, and our hearts become heavy. What's needed is plenty of rest, a large dose of perspective, and God's healing touch, but not necessarily in that order.

Today, why not claim the joy that is rightfully yours in Christ? Why not take time to celebrate God's glorious creation? Why not trust your hopes instead of your fears? When you do, you will think optimistically about yourself and your world, and you can then share your optimism with others. They'll be better for it, and so will you. But not necessarily in that order.

Heavenly Father, You love me, You care for me, and You protect me. You have given me the priceless gift of eternal life through the sacrifice that Christ made on the cross at Calvary. Because of You, Father, and because of Your Son, I can live each day with celebration in my heart and praise on my lips. Let me always be thankful, and let me share the Good News of Jesus as I turn my thoughts to You this day and always. Amen

PATIENCE

Rejoice in hope; be patient in affliction; be persistent in prayer.

Romans 12:12 HCSB

Love is patient; love is kind.

1 Corinthians 13:4 HCSB

A patient spirit is better than a proud spirit.

Ecclesiastes 7:8 HCSB

Therefore the Lord is waiting to show you mercy, and is rising up to show you compassion, for the Lord is a just God. Happy are all who wait patiently for Him.

Isaiah 30:18 HCSB

Be gentle to everyone, able to teach, and patient.

2 Timothy 2:23 HCSB

Are you a perfectly patient fellow? If so, feel free to skip the rest of this page. But if you're not, here's something to think about: If you really want to become a more patient person, God is ready and willing to help.

The Bible promises that when you sincerely seek God's help, He will give you the things that you need—and that includes patience. But God won't force you to become a more patient person. If you want to become a more mature Christian, you've got to do some of the work yourself—and the best time to start doing that work is now.

So, if you want to gain patience and maturity, bow your head and start praying about it. Then, rest assured that with God's help, you can most certainly make yourself a more patient, understanding, mature Christian.

―――――

It is wise to wait because God gives clear direction only when we are willing to wait.

Charles Stanley

―――――

Dear Lord, let me live according to Your plan and according to Your timetable. When I am hurried, Lord, slow me down. When I become impatient with others, give me empathy. Today, Lord, let me be a patient Christian, and let me trust in You and in Your master plan. Amen

God's Promises About . . .

PEACE

God has called us to peace.

1 Corinthians 7:15 NKJV

Live peaceful and quiet lives in all godliness and holiness.

1 Timothy 2:2 NIV

You, Lord, give true peace to those who depend on you, because they trust you.

Isaiah 26:3 NCV

And the peace of God, which transcends all understanding, will guard your hearts and your minds in Christ Jesus.

Philippians 4:7 NIV

Peace I leave with you, My peace I give to you; not as the world gives do I give to you. Let not your heart be troubled, neither let it be afraid.

John 14:27 NKJV

Sometimes, peace can be a scarce commodity in a demanding, 21st-century world. How, then, can we find the peace that we so desperately desire? By slowing down, by keeping problems in perspective, by counting our blessings, and by trusting God.

Dorothy Harrison Pentecost writes, "Peace is full confidence that God is Who He says He is and that He will keep every promise in His Word."

And Beth Moore advises, "Prayer guards hearts and minds and causes God to bring peace out of chaos."

So today, as you journey out into the chaos of the world, bring God's peace with you. And remember: the chaos is temporary, but God's peace is not.

The better you become acquainted with God, the less tensions you feel and the more peace you possess.

Charles L. Allen

Dear Lord, the peace that the world offers is fleeting, but You offer a peace that is perfect and eternal. Let me take my concerns and burdens to You, Father, and let me feel the spiritual abundance that You offer through the person of Your Son, the Prince of Peace. Amen

God's Promises About . . .

PERSEVERANCE

Do you not know that the runners in a stadium all race, but only one receives the prize? Run in such a way that you may win. Now everyone who competes exercises self-control in everything. However, they do it to receive a perishable crown, but we an imperishable one.

1 Corinthians 9:24-25 HCSB

But as for you, be strong; don't be discouraged, for your work has a reward.

2 Chronicles 15:7 HCSB

I have fought the good fight, I have finished the race, I have kept the faith.

2 Timothy 4:7 HCSB

So we must not get tired of doing good, for we will reap at the proper time if we don't give up.

Galatians 6:9 HCSB

Let us lay aside every weight and the sin that so easily ensnares us, and run with endurance the race that lies before us, keeping our eyes on Jesus, the source and perfecter of our faith.

Hebrews 12:1-2 HCSB

Are you one of those guys who doesn't give up easily, or are you quick to bail out when the going gets tough? If you've developed the unfortunate habit of giving up at the first sign of trouble, it's probably time for you to have a heart-to-heart talk with the guy you see every time you look in the mirror.

A well-lived life is like a marathon, not a sprint—it calls for preparation, determination, and lots of perseverance. As an example of perfect perseverance, you need look no further than your Savior, Jesus Christ.

Jesus finished what He began. Despite His suffering, despite the shame of the cross, Jesus was steadfast in His faithfulness to God. You, too, should remain faithful, especially when times are tough.

Are you facing a difficult situation? If so, remember this: whatever your problem, God can handle it. Your job is to keep persevering until He does.

Perseverance is more than endurance. It is endurance combined with absolute assurance and certainty that what we are looking for is going to happen.

Oswald Chambers

When I'm discouraged—or worse—let me turn to You, Lord for strength, for courage, and for love. Amen

PLEASING GOD

By an act of faith, Enoch skipped death completely. "They looked all over and couldn't find him because God had taken him." We know on the basis of reliable testimony that before he was taken "he pleased God."

Hebrews 11:5 MSG

I tried keeping rules and working my head off to please God, and it didn't work. So I quit being a "law man" so that I could be God's man. Christ's life showed me how, and enabled me to do it. I identified myself completely with him. Indeed, I have been crucified with Christ. My ego is no longer central.

Galatians 2:19-20 MSG

Everything that goes into a life of pleasing God has been miraculously given to us by getting to know, personally and intimately, the One who invited us to God. The best invitation we ever received!

2 Peter 1:3 MSG

Be energetic in your life of salvation, reverent and sensitive before God. That energy is God's energy, an energy deep within you, God himself willing and working at what will give him the most pleasure.

Philippians 2:12-13 MSG

In a scene from the movie "Chariots of Fire," a Scottish missionary named Eric Liddle explained why he was preparing to run in the 1924 Olympics. Liddle said that God had made him for a purpose: to be a missionary in China. But he added that God had also given him the ability to run fast. Liddle concluded by saying, "When I run, I feel God's pleasure."

God created you with a unique set of talents and opportunities. When you use those talents to the fullest, then you, like Liddle, may sense God's pleasure.

Marie Curie observed, "Life is not easy for any of us. But what of that? We must have perseverance and above all confidence in ourselves. We must believe that we are gifted for something and that this thing must be attained." And her words apply to you!

You must never sacrifice your relationship with God for the sake of a relationship with another person.

Charles Stanley

Lord, You know my heart, and you're concerned with the "inner me." Today, I will worry less about what other people think . . . and I'll worry more about what You think. Amen

God's Promises About . . .

PRAISE

I will praise You with my whole heart.

Psalm 138:1 NKJV

Is anyone happy? Let him sing songs of praise.

James 5:13 NIV

Through Him then, let us continually offer up a sacrifice of praise to God, that is, the fruit of lips that give thanks to His name.

Hebrews 13:15 NASB

Praise ye the LORD. O give thanks unto the LORD; for he is good: for his mercy endureth for ever.

Psalm 106:1 KJV

It is good to give thanks to the Lord, to sing praises to the Most High. It is good to proclaim your unfailing love in the morning, your faithfulness in the evening.

Psalm 92:1-2 NLT

I f you're like most guys on the planet, you're a very busy fellow. Your life is probably hectic, demanding, and complicated. When the demands of life leave you rushing from place to place with scarcely a moment to spare, you may fail to pause and thank your Creator for the blessings He has bestowed upon you. Big mistake.

No matter how busy you are, you should never be too busy to thank God for His gifts. Your task, as an extreme follower of the living Christ, is to praise God many times each day. After all, your Heavenly Father has blessed you beyond measure, and you owe Him everything, including your thanks, starting now.

———

Maintaining a focus on God will take our praise to heights that nothing else can.

Jeff Walling

———

Heavenly Father, I come to You today with hope in my heart and praise on my lips. I place my trust in You, Dear Lord, knowing that with You as my Protector, I have nothing to fear. I thank You, Lord, for Your grace, for Your love, and for Your Son. Let me follow in Christ's footsteps today and every day that I live. And then, when my work here is done, let me live with You forever. Amen

God's Promises About . . .

PRAYER

And everything—whatever you ask in prayer, believing—you will receive.

Matthew 21:22 HCSB

Rejoice always! Pray constantly. Give thanks in everything, for this is God's will for you in Christ Jesus.

1 Thessalonians 5:16-18 HCSB

Therefore I want the men in every place to pray, lifting up holy hands without anger or argument.

1 Timothy 2:8 HCSB

The intense prayer of the righteous is very powerful.

James 5:16 HCSB

Yet He often withdrew to deserted places and prayed.

Luke 5:16 HCSB

Okay, from the looks of things, you're an extremely busy guy. And perhaps, because of your demanding schedule, you've neglected to pay sufficient attention to a particularly important part of your life: the spiritual part. If so, today is the day to change, and one way to make that change is simply to spend a little more time talking with God.

Perhaps, on occasion, you may find yourself overwhelmed by the press of everyday life. Perhaps you may forget to slow yourself down long enough to talk with God. Instead of turning your thoughts and prayers to Him, you may rely upon your own resources. Instead of asking God for guidance, you may depend only upon your own limited wisdom. A far better course of action is this: simply stop what you're doing long enough to open your heart to God; then listen carefully for His directions.

In all things great and small, seek God's wisdom and His grace. He hears your prayers, and He will answer. All you must do is ask.

———

Dear Lord, make me a man of constant prayer. Your Holy Word commands me to pray without ceasing. Let me take everything to You. When I am discouraged, let me pray. When I am lonely, let me take my sorrows to You. And when I am joyful, let me offer up prayers of thanksgiving. In all things great and small, at all times, whether happy or sad, let me seek Your wisdom and Your grace . . . in prayer. Amen

God's Promises About . . .

Whatever you do, do all to the glory of God.

1 Corinthians 10:31 NKJV

You're sons of Light, daughters of Day. We live under wide open skies and know where we stand. So let's not sleepwalk through life . . .

1 Thessalonians 5:5-6 MSG

We look at this Son and see the God who cannot be seen. We look at this Son and see God's original purpose in everything created.

Colossians 1:15 MSG

To everything there is a season, a time for every purpose under heaven.

Ecclesiastes 3:1 NKJV

There is one thing I always do. Forgetting the past and straining toward what is ahead, I keep trying to reach the goal and get the prize for which God called me . . . .

Philippians 3:13–14 NCV

Life is best lived on purpose. And purpose, like everything else in the universe, begins with God. Whether you realize it or not, God has a plan for your life, a divine calling, a direction in which He is leading you. When you welcome God into your heart and establish a genuine relationship with Him, He will begin, in time, to make His purposes known.

Sometimes, God's intentions will be clear to you; other times, God's plan will seem uncertain at best. But even on those difficult days when you are unsure which way to turn, you must never lose sight of these overriding facts: God created you for a reason; He has important work for you to do; and He's waiting patiently for you to do it.

And the next step is up to you.

It's incredible to realize that what we do each day has meaning in the big picture of God's plan.

Bill Hybels

Dear Lord, I seek to live a meaningful life; I will turn to You to find that meaning. I will study Your Word, I will obey Your commandments, I will trust Your providence, and I will honor Your Son. Give me Your blessings, Father, and lead me along a path that is pleasing to You, today, tomorrow, and forever. Amen

SERVICE

So prepare your minds for service and have self-control. All your hope should be for the gift of grace that will be yours when Jesus Christ is shown to you.

1 Peter 1:13 NCV

There are different kinds of gifts, but they are all from the same Spirit. There are different ways to serve but the same Lord to serve.

1 Corinthians 12:4–5 NCV

Therefore, since we receive a kingdom which cannot be shaken, let us show gratitude, by which we may offer to God an acceptable service with reverence and awe . . . .

Hebrews 12:28 NASB

If they serve Him obediently, they will end their days in prosperity and their years in happiness.

Job 36:11 HCSB

Whoever serves me must follow me. Then my servant will be with me everywhere I am. My Father will honor anyone who serves me.

John 12:26 NCV

If you genuinely seek to discover God's unfolding purpose for your life, you must ask yourself this question: "How does God want me to serve others?"

Whatever your path, whatever your calling, you may be certain of this: service to others is an integral part of God's plan for your life. Christ was the ultimate servant, the Savior who gave His life for mankind. As His followers, we, too, must become humble servants.

Every single day of your life, including this one, God will give you opportunities to serve Him by serving His children. Welcome those opportunities with open arms. They are God's gift to you, His way of allowing you to achieve greatness in His kingdom.

No life can surpass that of a man who quietly continues to serve God in the place where providence has placed him.

C. H. Spurgeon

Dear Lord, let me help others in every way that I can. Jesus served others; I can too. I will serve other people with my good deeds and with my prayers. And I will give thanks for everybody who helps me. Amen

SIMPLICITY

"You've gotten a reputation as a bad-news people, you people of Judah and Israel, but I'm coming to save you. From now on, you're the good-news people. Don't be afraid. Keep a firm grip on what I'm doing."

Zechariah 8:12-13 MSG

But he's already made it plain how to live, what to do, what God is looking for in men and women. It's quite simple: Do what is fair and just to your neighbor, be compassionate and loyal in your love, and don't take yourself too seriously—take God seriously.

Micah 6:8 MSG

We brought nothing into the world, so we can take nothing out. But, if we have food and clothes, we will be satisfied with that.

1 Timothy 6:7-8 NCV

"I made all this! I own all this!" God's Decree. "But there is something I'm looking for: a person simple and plain, reverently responsive to what I say."

Isaiah 66:2 MSG

I s yours a life of moderation or accumulation? Are you more interested in the possessions you can acquire or in the person you can become? The answers to these questions will determine the direction of your day and, in time, the direction of your life.

Ours is a highly complicated society, a place where people and corporations vie for your attention, for your time, and for your dollars. Don't let them succeed in complicating your life! Keep your eyes focused instead upon God.

If your material possessions are somehow distancing you from God, discard them. If your outside interests leave you too little time for your family or your Creator, slow down the merry-go-round, or better yet, get off the merry-go-round completely. Remember: God wants your full attention, and He wants it today, so don't let anybody or anything get in His way.

It is part of Satan's program to make our faith complicated and involved. Now and then, we need a rediscovery of the simplicity that is in Christ and in our faith in Him.

Vance Havner

Dear Lord, help me understand the joys of simplicity. Life is complicated enough without my adding to the confusion. Wherever I happen to be, help me to keep it simple—very simple. Amen

God's Promises About . . .

SPIRITUAL GROWTH

Run away from infantile indulgence. Run after mature righteousness—faith, love, peace—joining those who are in honest and serious prayer before God.

2 Timothy 2:22 MSG

For You, O God, have tested us; You have refined us as silver is refined. You brought us into the net; You laid affliction on our backs. You have caused men to ride over our heads; we went through fire and through water; but You brought us out to rich fulfillment.

Psalm 66:10–12 NKJV

For this reason we also, since the day we heard it, do not cease to pray for you, and to ask that you may be filled with the knowledge of His will in all wisdom and spiritual understanding.

Colossians 1:9 NKJV

So let us stop going over the basics of Christianity again and again. Let us go on instead and become mature in our understanding.

Hebrews 6:1 NLT

The journey toward spiritual maturity lasts a lifetime. As Christians, we can and should continue to grow in the love and the knowledge of our Savior as long as we live. Norman Vincent Peale had simple advice for believers of all ages: "Ask the God who made you to keep remaking you." That advice, of course, is perfectly sound but too often ignored.

When we cease to grow, either emotionally or spiritually, we do ourselves and our families a profound disservice. But, if we study God's Word, if we obey His commandments, and if we live in the center of His will, we will not be "stagnant" believers; we will, instead, be growing Christians . . . and that's exactly what God wants for our lives.

In those quiet moments when we open our hearts to God, the Creator who made us keeps remaking us. He gives us direction, perspective, wisdom, and courage. And, the appropriate moment to accept His spiritual gifts is always this one.

———

Dear Lord, the Bible tells me that You are at work in my life, continuing to help me grow and to mature in my faith. Show me Your wisdom, Father, and let me live according to Your Word and Your will. Amen

God's Promises About . . .

TALENTS

According to the grace given to us, we have different gifts: If prophecy, use it according to the standard of faith; if service, in service; if teaching, in teaching; if exhorting, in exhortation; giving, with generosity; leading, with diligence; showing mercy, with cheerfulness.

Romans 12:6-8 HCSB

His master said to him, "Well done, good and faithful slave! You were faithful over a few things; I will put you in charge of many things. Enter your master's joy!"

Matthew 25:21 HCSB

Every good gift and every perfect gift is from above, and cometh down from the Father of lights.

James 1:17 KJV

Do not neglect the gift that is in you.

1 Timothy 4:14 HCSB

I remind you to keep ablaze the gift of God that is in you.

2 Timothy 1:6 HCSB

God gives us talents for a reason: to use them. Each of us possesses special abilities, gifted by God, that can be nurtured carefully or ignored totally. Our challenge, of course, is to use our talents to the greatest extent possible. But we are mightily tempted to do otherwise. Why? Because converting raw talent into polished skill usually requires work, and lots of it. God's Word clearly instructs us to do the hard work of refining our talents for the glory of His kingdom and the service of His people.

The old saying is both familiar and true: "What we are is God's gift to us; what we become is our gift to God." May we always remember that our talents and abilities are priceless gifts from our Creator, and that the best way to say "thank You" for those gifts is to use them.

If you want to reach your potential, you need to add a strong work ethic to your talent.

John Maxwell

Lord, You gave me talents and abilities for a reason. Let me use my talents for the glory of Your kingdom, and let me praise You always because You are the Giver of all gifts, including mine. Amen

God's Promises About . . .

TEMPTATION

No temptation has seized you except what is common to man. And God is faithful; he will not let you be tempted beyond what you can bear. But when you are tempted, he will also provide a way out so that you can stand up under it.

1 Corinthians 10:13 NIV

Be sober, be vigilant; because your adversary the devil walks about like a roaring lion, seeking whom he may devour.

1 Peter 5:8 NKJV

The Lord knows how to deliver the godly out of temptations.

2 Peter 2:9 NKJV

Put on the whole armor of God, that you may be able to stand against the wiles of the devil.

Ephesians 6:11 NKJV

This High Priest of ours understands our weaknesses, for he faced all of the same temptations we do, yet he did not sin.

Hebrews 4:15 NLT

Face the facts: you live in a temptation-filled world. The devil is hard at work in your neighborhood, and so are his helpers. Here in the 21st century, the bad guys are working around the clock to lead you astray. That's why you must remain vigilant.

In a letter to believers, Peter offers a stern warning: "Your adversary, the devil, prowls around like a roaring lion, seeking someone to devour" (1 Peter 5:8 NASB). What was true in New Testament times is equally true in our own. Satan tempts his prey and then devours them (and it's up to you—and only you—to make sure that you're not one of the ones being devoured!).

As a believer who seeks a radical relationship with Jesus, you must beware because temptations are everywhere. Satan is determined to win; you must be equally determined that he does not.

———

Lord, life is filled with temptations to stray from Your chosen path. But, I face no temptation that You have not already met and conquered through my Lord and Savior Jesus Christ, the One who empowers me with His strength and His love. Amen

WISDOM

Therefore everyone who hears these words of mine and puts them into practice is like a wise man who built his house on the rock.

Matthew 7:24 NIV

But the wisdom that is from above is first pure, then peaceable, gentle, willing to yield, full of mercy and good fruits, without partiality and without hypocrisy.

James 3:17 NKJV

Who is wise and understanding among you? Let him show by good conduct that his works are done in the meekness of wisdom.

James 3:13 NKJV

Let the word of Christ dwell in you richly in all wisdom; teaching and admonishing one another in psalms and hymns and spiritual songs, singing with grace in your hearts to the Lord.

Colossians 3:16 KJV

The fear of the Lord is the beginning of wisdom, and knowledge of the Holy One is understanding.

Proverbs 9:10 HCSB

Are you a wise guy? Hopefully, you're a very wise fellow who's getting wiser every day. But even if you're a very smart fellow, there's still lots more for you to learn. Wisdom is not like a dandelion or a mushroom; it does not spring up overnight. It is, instead, like an oak tree that starts as a tiny acorn, grows into a sapling, and eventually reaches up to the sky, tall and strong. To become wise, you must seek God's wisdom and live according to His Word. To become wise, you must seek wisdom with consistency and purpose. To become wise, you must not only learn the lessons of the Christian life, you must also live by them.

Are you passionate in your pursuit of God's wisdom? And do you sincerely seek to live a life of righteousness? If so, you must study the ultimate source of wisdom: the Word of God. You must seek out worthy teachers and listen carefully to their advice. You must associate, day in and day out, with godly friends. And, you must act in accordance with your beliefs. When you do these things, you will become wise . . . and you will be a blessing to your friends, to your family, and to the world.

Dear Lord, when I depend upon the world's wisdom, I make many mistakes. But when I trust in Your wisdom, I build my life on a firm foundation. Today and every day I will trust Your Word and follow it, knowing that the ultimate wisdom is Your wisdom and the ultimate truth is Your truth. Amen

God's Promises About . . .

WORRY

Jesus said, "Don't let your hearts be troubled. Trust in God, and trust in me."

John 14:1 NCV

Come to Me, all you who labor and are heavy laden, and I will give you rest. Take My yoke upon you and learn from Me, for I am gentle and lowly in heart, and you will find rest for your souls. For My yoke is easy and My burden is light.

Matthew 11:28-30 NKJV

Yea, though I walk through the valley of the shadow of death, I will fear no evil: for thou art with me; thy rod and thy staff they comfort me.

Psalm 23:4 KJV

Don't worry about anything, but in everything, through prayer and petition with thanksgiving, let your requests be made known to God.

Philippians 4:6 HCSB

If you are a man with lots of obligations and plenty of responsibilities, it is simply a fact of life: You worry. From time to time, you worry about health, about finances, about safety, about family, and about countless other concerns, some great and some small.

Where is the best place to take your worries? Take them to God. Take your troubles to Him; take your fears to Him; take your doubts to Him; take your weaknesses to Him; take your sorrows to Him . . . and leave them all there. Seek protection from the One who offers you eternal salvation; build your spiritual house upon the Rock that cannot be moved.

Perhaps you are uncertain about your future or your finances—or perhaps you are simply a "worrier" by nature. If so, it's time to focus less on your troubles and more on God's promises. And that's as it should be because God is trustworthy . . . and you are protected.

Lord, sometimes, I can't seem to help myself: I worry. Even though I know to put my trust in You, I still become anxious about the future. Give me the wisdom to trust in You, Father, and give me the courage to live a life of faith, not a life of fear. Amen